INVINCIBLE

TENSIONGENTRY

authorHOUSE®

AuthorHouse™
1663 Liberty Drive
Bloomington, IN 47403
www.authorhouse.com
Phone: 1-800-839-8640

First published by AuthorHouse   4/28/2010

ISBN: 978-1-4520-1298-8 (e)
ISBN: 978-1-4520-1262-9 (sc)
ISBN: 978-1-4520-1297-1 (hc)

Library of Congress Control Number: 2010905186

Printed in the United States of America
Bloomington, Indiana

This book is printed on acid-free paper.

Invincible Poem Reviews

And The gods Made Love
This was amazing.... how you developed this story line, never straying from the concept, from foreplay, to love making, to satisfaction, this was a supreme masterpiece!
Athena317
Indianapolis, Indiana

How do you evoke such powerful emotions? Everything I read I fall in love with. And that's not because of my love for the written word. The lord has blessed you with some crazy ink. I'm lovin' it, boy. XOXO
Ms King
Federal Way, Washington

Invincible
By the time I reach the last line of this poem, I do believe that the narrator is invincible.
Coyote Girl
Sparrow Creek, NM

Blazingly beautiful and powerful as usual. Peace & Love
Phavored
Detroit, MI

Tell Me How You Want It
Ahhhh, The King in a steamy sensual flow. I love when an artist can slip and slide in and out of styles and subject matter. Erotic poetry can become stiff and bumpy if not properly attended too. Kind of like a sultry high maintenance lover. You stroked this muses dream smoothly. I applaud you King T. Blessings.
DarkhunterC
St. Paul, MN

I want it just the way you described it. Definitely the foot massage. *Smile* Vivid images from these mini escapades.
BlessedOne
Love's Highway, GA

Mandela
I Have Appreciated... Studied... And Have Admired Nelson Mandela For Years.... Now That I Am Currently In Johannesburg, A Piece Of This Magnitude Not Only Hits Home.... But Leaves Me Awestruck At What The People Of This Land Have Overcome and Subsequently Achieved In Such A Short Period.... Mandela and What He Has Represented Is Worthy Of This Beautiful Tribute and The Praise Of All Who Believe In The Concept Of Freedom and Democracy!!!!!! BRILLIANT TRIBUTE!!!!!!
Chize65
Newport News, VA

Beautifully Written Tribute... now this gets your "pride" up... pride for my brother and sisters and what they endured and in turn overcame and "pride" for a true man of principle and the courageous way he stands on top of last century's best of best of humanity, including the inspiration to write this amazing piece... Mandela, yes of course, certainly indeed... thanks for caring and sharing!
2b2b2
Bronx, NY

Woman
To capture a woman's worth is sometimes hard to do. It's the simple things in women that have captured men's hearts in battle. I give you a standing ovation for this piece, bravo!!! Superb piece of poetry, well thought out and colorful, you painted a beautiful picture of what all women are.
Superb piece!
Icanprovuwrong
Norfolk, VA

Wow this was beautiful, made me smile. Made me think about some things, some things I already know of course. Amazing write!!!
Bronzen63
Rocky Mount, NC

Sleepless In Seattle
You told the biography of kurt kobain in ur own words, genius!
Cell
Spanish Harlem, NY

Revolutionary
Excellent write from a great revolutionary. Your vision and purpose is ink stained in every verse. Awesome!
Jewels4myking
Wilmington, DE

A lot of TRUTH and KNOWLEDGE was dropped into this write. Skillful simplistic depth of meaning defining those hiding their shameful wrongs in the left hand in hopes folk will only notice what they choose to expose in their right hand. Well done, piercing message.
Toban 41
Sacramento, CA

Let's Get Lost
Wow! Now that's hot! I had to catch my breath on that one. But... now you know... in the confessional?! That must be hella good sex! lol Very pleasurable write.
1touchoflove
Ellicott City, MD

Man U be playin 'with that all nite! What you been drinkin'? Pass it to me... Keep pushin'...
Seabe0604
Houston, TX

Oh damn... oh damn... this is so delicious. i wish i could lose myself this way... today... all day.
 Just because. I've been such a patient girl...too patient... and i deserve it. Wow.
Shibari
Boston, MA

Oh No He Didn't
WOW!!! One of the best lyrical flows i have read in a while and the wordplay is insane...this piece had me laughin'... i know you over there like, "who's your daddy, damn it who's your daddy"... great piece!
ori.GINA.lity
Angola

Hahahhaa... Man you got me dying over here... You are fierce King...
I love this...You are truly a word wiz, you know how to handle your
bizz... Undisputed champ... Much blessings.
Iyah Fiyah
Toronto, Ontario, Canada

The Trail Of Tears
Whoa... I am just plain SPEECHLESS... that is sooooo deep~ with an air
of truth that cuts to the core!!! Thanks for stepping up to the plate...
Speak!!! Reach!!! I applaud U!!! UmmmmMMMUAHHH!!!!
Terrybabes0705
Lititz, PA

Tell Me How You Want It
Um yes, i'll take savage rhythm for 500 Alex! Hot as always TG.
Athena317
Indianapolis, Indiana

One
Wowzers... This was tight as hell... Can I say HELL?? Anyhow... the
story should read...
In the beginning of time... then this poem.
Dade33056
Opa-Locka, FL

WTF were u when I was lacking inspiration? You've completely, and
utterly stolen my breath...I love the way u love...how u express that
love...love that you've shared that love with us... found my new
favorite.
Lyric1985
Sao Paulo, Brazil

To my beautiful and ever faithful love Sharon.
To the four corners of my heart
Milan, Latrice, Keena, and Ricky Lynn Bell Gentry.
To my mentors Gordon and Sue Johnston.
To my wonderful sister Inez and
courageous brother Alonzo.
To my valued friends Terry and Tom.
And to the memories of my mother Theloia,
my aunties Mattie, Mildred, Almedia, and Mary,
my grandmother Hattie Williams,
and beloved D.C. and Rosa Ross.
And lastly to my muse the Waterbead.
Thank you for all the love you have given me.
I love each of you with a great and never ending love.

Foreword

Invincible

I became acquainted with Tensiongentry, his prose, and poetry when he joined The Artist Lounge, the over 64,000 member online poetry site and forum that showcases some of today's best poets and writers. As proprietor of The Artist Lounge I became a fan after the first reading of Tensiongentry's work. Later I became a friend, then shortly afterward I adopted Tensiongentry as my brother out of respect and admiration for a unique fellow writer/poet. Needless to say, I read a lot of writers, poets, authors, lyricist, etc... And I can honestly say that Tensiongentry stands out amongst the massive talent I survey on a daily basis! His style, wordage, and easy flow always keeps the reader's attention.

Tensiongentry pens poetry and prose in a clear and concise fashion. Yet, with a flair all his own that illuminates and empowers. Be it life issues, historical, passionate erotica, love, dedications, revolution, metaphysical, or inspirational Tensiongentry writes impassioned verses that captivate, educate, incite, and entertain with wit and charm. "Invincible" a genuine penning from his heart, is empowering , enlightening and soul-stirring… a true page turner that will keep you enthralled. I am sure you will be, delighted, uplifted, and inspired by this book. Once you have read what Tensiongentry has stroked onto these pages you will agree that "Invincible" leaves the reader feeling invincible!

Jill Delbridge
Founder of The Artist Lounge
and radio host of Talkshoe

Poetry is a form of expression. It allows you to express how you feel and what you think. Essentially, to me, poetry let's you express who you are and what you are about artistically. Though I feel structure is necessary in poetry, I also feel that poetry should be free-flowing and unrestrictive. It doesn't have to rhyme. It doesn't need to have a certain writing style or a specific number of lines. The poem should conform to how the author sees fit. To me, poetry is personal and the purpose of it is to allow an individual to express themselves regardless of whose listening or reading. Poetry can lack structure and proper grammar, as long as the author feels that they have artistically accomplished their self expression. GS Poetry allows authors to write as they feel and as they think. It's raw, it's real and it's refreshing. The ability to come to a web site and write as you feel without being criticized by administrators or hearing that profanity is not allowed. Tensiongentry the author of Invincible is a GS Poetry member and his powerful writings reflect what GS Poetry is about with its ability to express love, passion, rage, wisdom, compassion, humor and sensuality with words and in a style that is truly gripping and artistically remarkable.

AC

GS Poetry Founder

Introduction

If something can make you happier and bring you more pleasure do you want it? Will you pass up something that makes you feel alive? Can you be disinterested in a source that makes you more aware of what is going on in the world around you as well as within you? Would you be afraid to touch something you knew would change your life, your way of thinking, your way of feeling, of acting and reacting? Will you shy away from something that opens a door to expand your capacity to love and be loved? Will you walk away from something guaranteed to make you tingle inside, run away from something that makes you feel more sensual and leads you to explore greater sexual landscapes? Can you refuse to experience a voice that connects you to a more intimate understanding of the creator of all life and his purpose for placing you in this world, on this planet, at this particular time? You are now holding the answers to these questions in your hands, your mind and your heart.

I have poured out my body, mind, soul and spirit into this book but that is not in itself extraordinary because any good writer does that. What is extraordinary is that I am inviting you to touch my heart while it is still beating freshly on the page. I am welcoming you inside my mind to taste and see the love, anger, passion, harmony, tragedy, hope, fears, and courage that have made me and continue to shape me by the hour, minute, and second. I am asking to hold your hand and allowing you to hold mine as we tear down the fortresses, overcome the obstacles, shed the inhibitions, set fire to the taboos, and destroy the myths men have constructed to try and keep us from becoming the persons we were created to be. I am looking into your eyes and letting you gaze directly into mine as I ask you to come away with me from the madness, and tyranny, and beauty and confusion of this world long enough to become my friend, comrade, pupil, or lover. I welcome you to experience me and ask for the pleasure of experiencing you.

It is my great desire that this book be more than just a book, that these words be more than just poetry. I want them to be a gateway, a portal that you can use to enter into a whole other world, a bridge you can use to cross over from the person you've become to reach the person you long to be. I want it to be a torch wives and husbands can use to reignite the flames of passion and love they felt when their love was new. I want it to be a roadmap for young lovers to stay on course and never let love become like stale bread or stagnant water. I want husbands to take time to read romantic and erotic passages from these pages to their wives to set the mood for evenings of romance and nights of pleasure. I want college professors to read excerpts from the militant poems to their students to let them know that they have a responsibility to mankind to always challenge conventional thinking and oppose wrong and oppression. I want parents to read passages to their teenagers to illustrate to them that life is a struggle but if they strive to be all they can be and stay true to their mission they will eventually win. And, I want people to read the poems, the stories, the experiences captured on these pages to encourage themselves in times of darkness and celebrate life in times of joy. I wish this book to be an Art of War and Kama Sutra for modern times. Open the cover of Invincible and breathe in the words, let them saturate you.

All this and more lay between the covers of this book awaiting your eyes, mind, inner ear and your heart to consume it and be consumed by it. In chapter one we will explore love in all its many forms. In chapter two we will journey the roads of life to see what it has taught me and what it is still teaching us. Chapter three will engulf you in the sensual, the sexy, the erotic where we will see lovers and be lovers. The fourth chapter will invite you to join forces with me to strike a blow against the wrongs and ills of this world and also conquer the enemy that is us. Chapter five will greet us with tributes to those who carved a unique place for themselves in history and in our hearts with their fabulous talents and amazing gifts. Finally in chapter six we will walk under the canopied sky of the grand finale to this journey and watch it conclude with verbal fireworks and literary explosions that will rock the foundations of your soul and leave you gasping for more of me and I longing for more of you. When you have melted into the last page you will know that you are both weaker and stronger than you think, poorer and richer, more earthly but much more beautiful than you ever imagined. When the last syllable disappears into your ear and drips from your lips you will truly understand why you are, I am, and we are INVINCIBLE.

Table of Contents

Chapter One:
Love and other Miracles

When love speaks, the voice of all the Gods
Makes heaven drowsy with the harmony.

William Shakespeare

And The gods Made Love

We are gods my love
you and I

You are thunder, earth shaking, vibrating
and I lightning, illuminating, penetrating
when the gateway of your love
opens wide to receive me
time stands frozen in anticipation
humanity is silenced into humble submission
as I circle, my love surrounding you
deliciously assailing you from every angle
when we are joined together
it is a spectacle to behold
angels hover above us bug-eyed
beating their wings in ecstasy
when we come together
it is a force stronger than nature
a gravitational pull that cannot be refused
a sonic boom within the room, like worlds colliding

When the moment arises
you are locked in my embrace
joyously beneath the weight of me
like the earth beneath the stars
hearts beating like savage drums
candles casting our shadows against the wall
reflections captured in the mirror of our eyes
your body screaming out sweet melodies
mine shouting back beautiful harmonies
heavenly chorus ringing in our ears
comingling to create the perfect soundtrack
recalling memories of the first time
knowing there will never be a last time
You are wine poured out for me
I am bread broken for you
we are a banquet, a love feast

We are gods my love
and when we unite it is
as the birthing of queens and pharaohs
the melting of glaciers
explosions on the surface of the sun
tongue licking, pulse quickening
flesh slapping together like the crack of a whip
fitting together like vice and grip
making mountains rumble, planets tumble
the earth slide off its axis
the four winds break loose from their moorings
to go hurtling into the vastness of space
volcano erupting, lava flowing
universe expanding, growing, glowing
all the while knowing this is but foreplay
a prelude to our saucy screenplay

Ballet becomes hip-hop
drip drops of sweat on our skin glistening
the world now listening to our jubilant song
coordination, elation to show and tell
positioning, the conditioning that serves us well
precision, the rhythm of magnificent machines
If you are willing, let's go drilling into the core
steeper, deeper than ever before
clumps of jelly we shiver and shake
quiver and quake, we give and we take
sirens blaring in our veins
we moan and groan, we stretch and strain
consumed by this fire we ignited
abandoning these masks designed to hide
the primal urge we feel inside
to throw ourselves into the flames

Now the climax within reach
as sand upon a moonlit beach
waves of pleasure wash us over
your cheek buried against my shoulder
head tossing from left to right

but still the bliss will not subside
your body balanced on pleasure's peak
and I unable to even speak
caught inside the undertow
we push and pull until we flow
like rivers emptying into the sea
I cling to you, you cling to me
and when the night becomes the dawn
awakening in each other's arms
with passion's kiss the day begins
this know before we start again

We are gods my love
you and I
yes, love gods.

One

There was you
then there was me
lost in the sea of our loneliness
drowning beneath the waves of misery
but now we are together
the pen of life is placed in our hands
we are one
and the writing of the story of our love
has just begun

Before the foundations of time were laid
and the universe constructed
before the earth was set upon its axis
and the four winds commanded to blow
you were created for me and I for you
the creator molded you and crafted you especially
so that every part of you fits every inch of me
that's why when I behold you
I love everything I see
we were created to be together
amen to amen eternally

I know you've been lonely
I been lonely too
I know your heart's been broken
I was broken too
I know there were times you wondered
would you ever feel me in your arms
while every trial, circumstance, and experience
was leading me to where you are
come let me massage your body
and relieve the stress
let my love overflow your cup
until it drives out the emptiness
all your desires and each and every fantasy
I was created to fill and created to be
come lay inside my fire

let it melt your every fear
you never have to cry another lonely tear
it took a long time but baby now I'm here

The sun and moon and the stars
were made to shine on us
the wind and the waves and the rain
are sent to remind us
how once we were sinking in darkness
not a speck of hope to be found
I reached out for you
you reached out for me
we found strength in each other's arms
now nothing can pull us down
there was a time you walked alone
now there's two footprints in the sand
there were nights
you longed to be touched
now you feel the caress
of my burning hands
you prayed for someone
to protect, to provide, make you feel alive
now I'm your strong tower
your financial power
your reason to breathe
the one
who makes passionate love to you
in the midnight hours
in the shower
brings you flowers

What shall I call you?
I will call you
my queen, my empress
sculpture of loveliness
my bright morning star
answer to my desires
the very air I breathe
bearer of my seed

the first face i want to see when i rise
and the last before I say goodnight
embodiment of sexiness
my lover victorious
my beautiful and glorious
everything love could possibly be
my every want my every need
and yes I'm here to bring you bliss
no there will be no end to this
I'm gonna stay right here never disappear
let the storms rage i don't care
I ain't goin' nowhere without you

Your lips are known to me
your hips are home to me
your breasts are my nectar
gonna keep workin' my love magic on you
until its perfected
ain't nobody gonna take my love
cain't nobody ever break our love
I was created just to give you love
feel so elated to receive your love
bring your body here to me
let me show you how deep love can be
let my river flow into your sea
until we are one
and you can't tell you from me
give me your mind let me explore it
until I understand who you are
what you want and what you need
so I can adore it
you can pour out your heart to me
I'm here to end the misery
you can cry on my shoulder
then lay back and let me hold ya
let me prove there's power in these rings
let me fine tune your body until it sings
whisper sexy things into your ear
kiss away your every salty tear

let me draw you so close to me
the sound of your heart beat
is distinctly clear
girl I'm here
to pacify, to electrify, to satisfy
your every fantasy
you can place your trust in me
let me light your candle with my flame
use my liquid fire
to quench your burning desires
touch you with the thunder of my love
fill you with the wonders of my love
are you ready
are you willing
because I'm more than able

First there was you
now there is me
and together forever
one in love we will be
take me by the hand
you're my woman I'm your man
we gonna seek we gonna reach
until we find our promised land
We Are One.

Still My Girl

If i could capture perfection in a picture frame
every picture on the wall would bear your name
if they gave medals for a pretty face
you'd be the only one sittin' in first place
i thought the sun rose and sat in your eyes girl
thought you would always be only my girl
love is special when you lovin' for the first time
it's so strong it can get you through the worst times

Use to show up at your window and
knock knock
yo momma swore i was the baddest on the
block block
you showed love let me eat out of the
pot pot
when you married him you know i was in
shock shock

Now i hear you back at your momma's place
after four years you wish you could erase
feelin' down cause you fell on hard times
don't forget you still a friend of mine
don't hang your head when you see me on the street
don't have to wait til you back on your feet
I'm not the kind that forgets what you done for me
you need somethin' you can always run to me

Show up at my door all you gotta do is
knock knock
even though i'm still bout the baddest on the
block block
come over tonight we can eat straight out the
pot pot
If i say I love you don't let it be a
shock shock

There are some things never seem to fade away
like the times we'd go swimmin' on a summer day
all week savin' bottles for a picture show
sneak a kiss when the lights went down low
walkin' home past the thugs in the neighborhood
they let us be cause they knew we understood
don't trip when folks talk behind your back
remember i'm still the same damn one that

Showed up at your window every day with a
knock knock
the one momma swore was the baddest on the
block block
still you showed love let me eat out of the
pot pot
that's why baby girl i'll give you all i
got got.

Message From The Road

Though the road is long
I am coming home...

But if I lose my way
will you find me
can you help me leave the past
far behind me
I am reaching out to you
please remind me
of what I had before
when love was so much more

With open arms
and wounded heart
and many tears
I run to you
I'm broken
and I'm tired
but determined
to come to you
this pain inside
I cannot hide
can't wait til I
find rest in you
help me find my way
don't let me go astray

And if the darkness falls
before I get there
will you wait for me
until I get there
knowing I am on my way
and when I get there
I will come out of the storm
to take you in my arms

Through space and time
and a world gone blind
darling I
I run to you
though battered
and shattered
into a million pieces
I come to you
I'm trying
and I'm crying
girl I'm dying
just to be with you
can you stop the pain
help me live again

I am so afraid
I will lose you
and it took so long
just to find you
so if life's journey ends
before touching you again
know that it was you
I was running to

I'm breathless
and I'm reckless
but through all this
I run to you
I'm falling
sometimes crawling
hear me calling
as I come to you
through the sadness
and the madness
still I know this
I am one with you
I am scattered like the rain
can you make me whole again

All my heart is yours
please receive it
one day we'll be one
if you believe it
when that day is here
to celebrate it
let my gift from you
be that you love me too

I'm breathless
and I'm reckless
but through all this
I run to you
I'm falling
sometimes crawling
hear me calling
as I come to you
through the sadness
and the madness
still I know this
I am one with you
though the road is long
until I make it home...

My gift to you is love.

Lover Please

Lover Please
forgive the wrong I've done
lover please
wait til morning comes
lover please
please don't say we're done
tell me love can find a way

You can't mean the things you say
wait til the light of day
search til we find a way
don't turn and walk away
give me a chance I pray
to make this all ok
all that we cannot say
leave til another day

Lover Please
put your fears away
lover please
I'm begging you to stay
lover please
don't throw our love away
not after all we been through

Put down your bags and wait
tell me it's not too late
I'll send the cab away
don't test the hand of fate
just let me concentrate
I promise I'll find a way
to clean up the mess I've made
don't use the word hate

Lover Please
find no pleasure when I fall
lover please

do you wanna make me crawl
lover please
if you care for me at all
let me make this up to you

Pause just to think awhile
give just a little smile
no I'm not in denial
I'll make it right somehow
we've come so far but I'll
go just another mile
though crying is not my style
my tears are flowing like the Nile

Don't you see
I'm sorry I put you through this
I beg you please
lover don't you do this
If you leave
how will I get through this
your loss will be the death of me

We were so in harmony
but now that you've gone from me
pain is the melody
that plays on my agony
your love took the best of me
this is all that's left of me
if you can't come back to me
at least haunt my memories.

Warning: Handle With Extreme Care

You say you love me
i know it's true
so it's only fair i warn you
before you touch me
dare to love me
place your trust and hopes upon me
careful how you ignite my desires
my love's an all consuming fire
i'm a human praying mantis
the kind of love that sunk Atlantis
i'm the yin and the yang
i will seep into your brain
abduct your heart steal your mind
make you lose both place and time
til you cannot live without me
can't stop thinking about me
i'll get ingested into your lungs
and spread like a weed
until i am the molecules
of the very air you breathe
i'm an hourly addiction
a love disease with no prescription
i'm a slinky velvet rope
love poison with no antidote
way past the point of no return
i'm the lesson never learned
a tragedy, a comedy
my energy will make you run to me
i'm an ocean
get out before you're in too deep
i'm a mountain
turn back before the climb's too steep
my love's highly combustible
my heart is unadjustible
the intent of my propensity
is to suck you completely into me

Once the taste of my love
hits the tip of your tongue
you'll be hooked like a fish
dazed and wondering
what you've become
when your lovely eyes behold me
you'll always want to hold me
spend afternoons with me
spoon with me
journey the earth and moon with me
my arms will be the cradle
you long to rock you
my %#&@$! will be the only one
you want to %#&@$! you
only trying to let you know
you'll never want to let me go
your will power will hit the door
i'll make you lose self control
you'll think you've died
and went to heaven
you'll want to ride me
24/7
i'll lodge inside your brain cells
get stuck under your fingernails
ring you like a church bell
do things to you, you can't tell
pour my love on you like drenching rain
sweep you off your feet like a hurricane
you'll want no other hands to touch you
no other man to love you
i'll be the earth beneath your feet
the sky above you
i'm a habit an addiction
half fantasy half science fiction
i'll flip you on like a light switch
turn past lovers into wreckage
take your body places it's never been
shoot you into outer space
then reel you in

i'll pop you like a toaster
thrill you like a roller coaster
heat your oven like a roaster
nail you to me like a poster
i will scour you devour you
use my tongue to shower you
lick you up lick you down
pick you up and swirl you round

If what i say doesn't scare you
like a trophy still you want me
girl i dig you like a shovel
let's take it to another level
be sure to follow my instructions
when we gettin' busy
when the room starts spinning
and your head is dizzy
it's alright hold on tight
squeeze my waist with all your might
let your fantasies take flight
watch the day turn into night
see the stars how they shine
drink my love like it's wine
you'll be fine take your time
this is how i make you mine
understand i'm a brand
in my eyes read the label
just a drop of me is needed
cause my love is concentrated
let's begin soak me in
where no other love has been
once i'm in let it go
surrender body mind and soul
it's alright you can cry
you are safe with me tonight
soar the heights climb the walls
i will never let you fall
touch the planets all the stars
there goes Jupiter and Mars

do you love me
you're breathing heavy
i'll slow it down and keep it steady
i'm your soldier hug my shoulder
no, the pleasure's far from over
make you squeal
you know i will
girl my love is hard as steel
you got walls?
i'll break through
this is what i'm born to do
the real you is locked inside
you can run but you can't hide
you've been invisible but girl i see you
and tonight i'm here to free you
feel the flow let it go
feels so good yes i know
say it's just the way you dreamed it
i don't mind you can scream it

In these arms you belong
yes it's lasting oh so long
yes you do, you excite me
it's alright go head and bite me
i can feel you you're exploding
let it take you i won't break you
let it shake you like a leaf
bring your body sweet release
you ask what i've done to you
it's just love you never knew
you've crossed the line
heart open wide
can't go back to the other side
i tried to make you aware
my love is more than truth or dare
baby handle with extreme care
before you step off in here
cause once i shot you
girl i got you

ain't no turnin' back about this
you'll never want to live without this
i'll gobble you up like Reese's Pieces
have my love oozing from all your creases
i tried to warn you no one can beat me
now you belong to me completely.

The Light In The Window

There is an open window
where a solitary candle flickers in the wind
enduring no matter how late the hour
as the cold chill of winter spreads
a blanket of dew on the green grass
announcing summer has silently headed south
leaving behind what it could not take
on a hopeful but lonely flight
swollen eyes roaming, searching for a warmer home
for the peace and comfort of a better place
where dreams can be realized
and budding prospects can blossom and bloom

There is no need to chase the past my love
where memories fog the mind
shrouding both what is before and behind
what is done is gone and best forgotten
for wanting without possessing is emptiness
for who can recapture things undone
reclaim words unsaid
let that which you possess be enough
let life's compass point you toward home
where there are flames in the fireplace
ample food on the kitchen table
and inviting covers are turned down and waiting

Sometimes our desires outdistance our needs
the hunger for more deprives us of simple pleasures
for the heart is indeed a lonely hunter
crying together is better than laughing alone
restless one make your peace with yesterday
everything and nothing are what we make them
the light in the window still burns
there is nothing more to prove
your absence has clearly shown
love is not an island
and while all roads may lead to Rome

only one ushers you home

Bring your travels to an end
you have overturned every stone
in search of the illusive happiness you seek
you have reached the proverbial end of the road
turn now and peer down the deserted path
abandoned long ago and you will see
there is a light burning in the window
follow its glow to the house at the trail's end
and when you stand upon the welcome mat
don't knock because the door is never locked
just open it and come inside my love
for you are home.

The Black Knight

Against those who oppose us
and in the darkness conspire
to overthrow our kingdom
and quench our desires
I give you my allegiance
pledge my solemn word
I will never betray you
for the pleasures of this earth
I have taken an oath
your honor to defend
against those who would destroy you
be they gods or be they men
I have vowed to be with you
serve you with all my might
and I will uphold that vow
though it cost me my life

My eyes are ever vigilant
to protect you from harm
horizon to horizon
through the fierceness of the storm
rest assured my chosen queen
I will never leave your side
I am the guardian of love
your gallant black knight
if any dare injure
but a hair on your head
they will taste of my vengeance
before the sun is put to bed
I will ride upon lightning
to the place where they've fled
and my sword shall devour
til my justice is fed

When the armies of jealousy
that do plot your demise
gather to march against you

with their legion of lies
though they number against us
a thousand soldiers to one
I will ride out to meet them
beneath the shadow of their tongues
with my two edged sword
I will cut their lies into
with arrows of revelation
I will pierce them with truth
when the conflict has ended
and the victory is won
let me wash my battle scars
in the river of your arms

Upon the waves of the oceans
the sizzling desert sands
the frigid mountain peaks
the scattered islands
as far as the eagle flies
and the great lion prowls
my love for you is infinite
it will know no bounds
through 100,000 nights
and as many passing days
I will live within your eyes
and to gaze upon your face
summer's heat winter's cold
spring blossoms frost of fall
my unwavering devotion for you
will endure them all

When mortality invades us
with the certainty of defeat
I will never surrender
I will never retreat
I will hold my position
wage my desperate fight
eternal is the mission
of this gallant black knight

in the corridor of memories
I will make my last stand
before the chamber of your heart
for the glory of your hand
when finally overrun
by the armies of death
your name shall be on my lips
when I draw my last breath.

The Sea of Love

New love is a calm sea not meant to expose
weakness and flaws of heart and soul
but time is a tempest whose wind and rain
inspects dear lovers from bow to stern
exploits each crack with drips and leaks
which collect into a deadly flood
that drags the vessel to the floor
of what was once a sea of love
and when the wreckage lay submerged
beneath dark rage and bitterness
some ask what brought the ship to ruin
poor craftsmanship and nothing less

Though rocky neglect damaged her hull
making her list toward foreign shores
harsh words beat upon her swollen decks
until they buckled under the weight
sails ripped by infidelity
could not catch wind to maintain pace
impatience rendered her rudderless
adrift and unable to change course
still she could have reached her port
had builders from birth bestowed their best
what reason then lay she on the bottom
poor craftsmanship and nothing less

And so dear lovers choose strongest timber
to withstand the inevitable storms of life
make firm but flexible your sails
to capture the fortunes of changing times
build your rudder of sturdy trust
whose hinges will not succumb to doubt
and all these mold with patience and compassion
knowing the hastily constructed litter the depths
respect and concern and endless passion
these are materials that will stand the test
for to navigate the sea of love
you must build your vessel on nothing less

I'm Your Man

You got the kind of body I dream of
but it ain't always about just makin' love
I hear you been goin' through some changes
I can tell by your tears how deep the pain is
just want you to know I'm here for you
always keep my calendar clear for you
don't be afraid to call me on the phone
long as I breathe you'll never be alone

Need someone to hold your hand
I'm Your Man
Need someone to understand
I'm Your Man
Need a shoulder to cry on
I'm Your Man
Need someone to rely on
I'm Your Man

He's always bringing you gifts and pretty things
yet he don't give you the love you really need
he talks about you like you ain't good enough
how could he fail to see you're a diamond in the rough
always pointing out what you're not baby
but he don't realize what he's got maybe
if he weren't so busy doin' his own thing
he'd see the girl on his arm is a true queen

Need someone to hold your hand
I'm Your Man
Need someone to understand
I'm Your Man
Need a shoulder to cry on
I'm Your Man
Need someone to rely on
I'm Your Man

I admit I don't know how you deal wit it
don't wanna hurt you but I gotta be real wit it
if you were mine this drama would be over
I'd love you girl til hell freezes over
don't wanna pressure you know you don't need that
just wanna be the one that you contact
not tellin' you that you should leave boo
but if you do I'm here to receive you

Need someone to hold your hand
I'm Your Man
Need someone to understand
I'm Your Man
Need a shoulder to cry on
I'm Your Man
Need someone to rely on
I'm Your Man

Baby, I'm Your Man.

The Wonders of My Love

Give me the chance to be
everything you need
through the wonders of my love
you will see...

I'll be your Grand Canyon
my love will run so deep and span so wide
i'll be your place to run and hide
I'll be your Wall of China
my arms will surround you always embrace you
keep you safe and warm inside
I'll be your Mt. Everest
a towering love to show you heights of passion
you've never reached before
I'll be a Taj Mahal
your monument of love existing just to prove
no one else can love you more

Give me the chance to be
everything you need
through the wonders of my love
you will see...

I'll be your Tower of Pisa
no matter where you go I'll make sure my love
leans in your direction
I'll be the Colloseum
your gladiator of love go to work each day
to fight for your protection
I'll be your Stonehenge
my love will be a mystery you'll never be tired of me
we'll grow old together
I'm your Pyramid of Giza
my love will endure through the end of time
I will be your shelter

Give me the chance to be
everything you need
through the wonders of my love
you will see
I will always love
you.

I Can Make It Rain

For years you watched the clouds roll by
none caring enough to ease your pain
loneliness like a blazing sun upon your heart
withered your hope until nothing remained
the scorched seed of your dreams cry out
for the nourishing rain it so desperately needs
but not a drop of rain comes down
before the clouds disappear from view

One day on the horizon a solitary cloud
separates from the others and turns your way
it closes the distance between you
and suddenly is directly overhead
he surveys the parched earth below
as dust blows across your forgotten plain
obscuring the beauty beneath the surface
but the cloud proclaims

I Can Make It Rain
I Can Make It Rain
I can make your love flower and bloom
I Can Make It Rain
I Can Make It Rain
I can soak your heart with tender loving dew
I can wash away all your hurt and pain
make your love grow and flourish again
I Can Make It Rain
I Can Make It Rain

For years no one paused to admire
the wilderness you became
as the passage of time eroded away
the fertile soil of your soul
you hoped and prayed someday
someone would care for you
but the sun beat down so harshly
your desire for love wilted and died

Then one day your cloud appeared
seeing you in the distance all alone
when he examined you closely he discovered
an oasis just waiting to bloom
he knew if the water he carried
could embrace you day and night
your emotions so hardened and wasted
would be fertile again

I Can Make It Rain
I Can Make It Rain
I can make your love flower and bloom
I Can Make It Rain
I Can Make It Rain
I can soak your heart with tender loving dew
I can wash away all your hurt and pain
make your love grow and flourish again
I Can Make It Rain
I Can Make It Rain.

No Reply

Woke this morning thinkin'
how'd i get here
looked in the mirror
and it was clear
I was stuck on the corner
of selfish greed
instead of coming back home
to the love I need
girl we felt so right
but it turned out wrong
now the days are short
and my nights are long
some days i smile
but not for long
hard to find the strength
to carry on

Never
should have let me taste you
knowing
no one could replace you
with each
memory i pay the cost
wishing
to gain back the love i lost

Your love is
one part physical
one part spiritual
one part sexy
and one part miracle

You told me I'd miss you
when you go
but I didn't hear
cause my ears are slow
but now you're gone

and I know you're rare
as a dollar in the pocket
of a billionaire

Your kiss is nonerasable
your body irreplaceable
missing you has taught me
what makes you irresistible

Uh oh
think i made a big mistake
tell me
how long will it take
to make you love me once again
now that our love is at an end

Counting memories like pennies
in a penny jar
no matter where you go
wanna be where you are
in the land of women
you're a superstar
only your forgiveness
can remove my scars
saw you the other day
and went to speak
but you turned your head
and crossed the street
call you on the phone
but you won't say hi
even sent you an email
but no reply

Our love was
one part physical
one part spiritual
but now that you've left
i'm all parts miserable

My heart begged me
to make you stay
but my pride just watched you
walk away
and now that my eyes
see what I've lost
my head is making me
pay the cost
not a day goes by
i swear it's true
something don't remind me
of lovin' you

Your voice is unerasable
smile irreplaceable
had the best and now i know
no one else can make me whole

Uh oh
think i made a big mistake
tell me
how long it will take
to make you love me once again
now that our love is at an end

If I thought this is how
it's supposed to be
and knew you weren't
coming back to me
i'd find myself
an ocean deep
and drown myself
in the salty sea
or find the highest
mountain top
climb day and night
til i reach the top
then shout your name
so the world can hear

how much it hurts
when you're not here

How could
you let me make love to you
Knowing
i'd get addicted to
the way
you move when we're front to back
now this
habit got me bout to crack

if there's a doctor in the house
come right away
i can tell my heart
is about to break
you stamped
your love on my very soul
now this pain I feel
is out of control

So baby can we
wake up make up
anything but break up
i'll learn to wash your hair
even do your make-up
anything to make you
come back to me
i once was blind
but now i swear i see

life's got more colors
than black and white
see my white flag wavin'
cause you won the fight
i'll send you an email
again tonight
please don't let it come back
no reply.

Will You Love Me

When the last tide has returned to the sea
and the last sun has shined it's light on me
when the last breeze has blown across my face
and my last smile has finally been erased
when my time reaches the end my love
will you love me then

When the chorus fades and my final note is sung
when the battle is over and my final deed is done
and all that I fought for is all that is left
when my heartbeat is silenced and I draw my last breath
when these words I have written are your only friend
will you love me then

I have given all my love to you
done the very best that I could do
so if this is goodbye
the story of a life
tell me before it ends
will you love me then

When the last day has dawned and the night closes in
when these arms that have held you cannot hold you again
when these lips you have kissed are frozen still
and I've heard the last robin on our windowsill
when this laugh that you love to hear
stops ringing in your ears
will you love me then

When you cry and I can no longer wipe your tears
when your phone doesn't ring cause I'm no longer here
when you walk our favorite path but you walk alone
your heart breaks each night because I'm not coming home
when only my memory quiets the pain within
will you love me then

I have given all my love to you
done the very best that I could do
if this is where the end starts
before I depart
tell me from your heart
will you love me then

When the first thing friends ask is how you been
when you feel like your heart can never love again
when our favorite songs always make you cry
when you must keep on living but you don't know why
when the moments we shared cause your soul to rend
will you love me then

I am forever by your side if only in spirit
whispering I love you listen to the wind and you will hear it
every time you feel the sun it's me kissing your face
wrapped in your blanket at night is my warm embrace
I will watch over you from above to keep you safe from harm
so if you love me then

lay your sweet head down to rest
knowing that we have done our best
to build a love that will stand the test
until time has passed us by
darling hold the tears you cry
until you meet me in the sky
I have loved you all my life
and I will love you even then.

Chapter Two:
Life, Death and
Everything Between

*As far as we can discern, the sole purpose
of human existence is to kindle a light in the
darkness of mere being.*

Carl Jung

Woman

Woman
they have bewitched you
with their smoke and mirrors
to the point where
you look in your mirror
and cannot see who you are
only who you are not
they shorten your dress
and expose your cleavage
put you in low riding jeans
revealing your derriere
as the split peaks over your waistband
and when you have left nothing
to the imagination
they tell you that is sexy

No my darling,
sexy is the vision you present
when you are fully clothed
leaving me to wonder
what treasures are buried beneath
for you are as tempting
draped in one of my oversized work shirts
as in your red satin and lace negligee
you slay me not with your eagerness to reveal
but with the mysterious way you conceal
not with the way you jiggle when you walk
but with a simple smile, intelligent conversation
and just your presence

Legs as long as a thoroughbred's
or short as a basset hound
big breasted, flat chested
bosoms full enough to fill a bucket
or slight enough to fit into a thimble
noses wide, or long, or thin
flowing locks and ebullient curls

skull tight afros or no hair at all
hips curvaceous as Mulholland Drive
or streamline as a swizzle stick
lips thick as T-bone steaks
or thin as wheat crackers

You are beautiful my darling
not as a result of Maybeline
Clairol, Tiffany
or some male fashion guru
nor as the result of thigh masters
ab rockers or Victoria's Secret
weight wachers, slim fast, Adkins
or Jenny Craig
liposuction, lap-bands, collagen
or the surgeon's knife
you are beautiful because
you are a woman

I value what you have to offer
in the boardroom
as much as what you have to offer
in the bedroom
whether in the kitchen preparing
Peking Duck and fried chicken
or in the garage
changing the oil or spark plugs
I am fascinated by your every move
interested in your every thought
you make each location more exotic
each vacation more erotic
every moment more memorable
every hardship more bearable
with you cold winter nights
become warm and inviting
hot summer days
turn cool and relaxing
experience has taught me
time away from you will be far too long

time alone with you will be much too short

I have come to realize
you are part magician
able to make time fly by or stand still
with a wink of your eye
part electrician
able to turn me on with just a glance
part physician
able to heal my deepest wounds
with a few thoughtful words

and part engineer
able to bridge the gap between us
with the span of your embrace
like a master architect
you renovate our relationship
ever turning what is old and familiar
into something fresh and alive

Just as you are
you are enough to make any man
let down his draw bridge, drain the mote
and unconditionally surrender all
there is no scale that can measure your worth
no currency that can exceed your value
no flower that can match your beauty
no boundaries to limit your compassion
what fortress can withstand your love
and what language convey your importance
no words can express emotions deep enough
no bird can sing a song sweet enough
without you the earth is uninhabitable
man's existence void and meaningless
I am told of all His creations
God saved the best for last
Woman
you are and always will be
worth the wait.

You're Nobody 'Til Somebody Hates You

What have you done
that heaven and earth revile you
that living and dead
speak your name only in hushed echoes
and malevolent tones
how have you fallen oh son of morning
that you can never stand in their presence
ever recapture your seat in their hearts

Beloved friend
son, daughter, father, mother, neighbor
the face that puts the smile
on the face
of loved ones, dear ones, relatives, fans
even strangers
this I know to be true
you're nobody til somebody hates you

Daddy's little princess
momma's pride and joy
everyone's hero
will never know the acclaim
nor ever draw the ire
can never set the world afire
just walking into a room
where they gather to defame

Embers smolder at the sight of you
combust into flames
race across carpet and up drapes
engulfing lamps, chairs, conversations
sucking the air from shrinking rooms
till all are gasping for breath
running from the blackened death
they heap upon your head

Until you are
the target of vicious attacks
caught in the crossfire
of clattering clacking tongues
that tear to shreds and chew into tiny bits
to spew paralyzing unsympathizing venom
into your gumbo life stew
you're nobody til somebody hates you

Until your reputation is tarnished
hacked to death and dismembered
good intentions, apologies, and explanations
dragged into plain view of the world
then set ablaze before their merciless gaze
ones who will never forgive
though your shrieks and tears
paint the walls a dehumanized hue

No fame or fortune can be as strong
last as long, expanding with time
boiling, baking under noonday sun
twilight's glow, midnight hour when all is black
contempt for you does not slack or sleep
ill wishes running fathoms deep
swelling into an ocean of hate
fed by rivers of lies, tributaries of unmet promises

None can rescue from this banished place
the play is cast and you are villain
monster, specter, hideous to behold
the sight of you sickens, quickens the pace
of the heart that harbors festering wounds
like spilled blood drying on simmering pavement
never to be restored to hollow vein
once a symbol of life, now a sign of death

Your name henceforth banned from lips
face stolen from memory banks
forever to represent

serpent, reptile, poisonous snake
all that is evil, wretched, and vile
putrid and metastasized
capsulized and magnified
you are the embodiment of every mistake

Try as you may to be glorious
win battles victorious
scale mountains unmeasurable
capture the imaginations
of man, woman and child
no conquest can etch in the mind as deep
you're never as unforgettable
as when you become regrettable
You're nobody til somebody hates you.

The Sun Also Rises

Hemingway said the sun also rises
I know this to be true
though I've had to remind myself of it
a thousand times
as dire situations and circumstances
ate at me like canker worms
undercutting the foundation of my soul
eroding the principles of life, liberty and the pursuit of...
like the muddy Mississippi
gnawing at its banks
dragging sediment as it goes
only to deposit it in a place even more barren
Why? Because this is the course of things
is the course chosen for me
before the creation of all that exist
from amen to amen

Was it predestination I be born of seed
generations removed from the belly of the beast
where they pitching and roiling in their own blood
and vomit and urine and feces and tears
chanting a language that would be lost to me
bound together by ancestry and chains
those who would donate their bodies to the sea
encased in the same compact hell
as those who would live to wish themselves dead
but could not die because it was their destiny
to give the world Frederick, and Carver
and Langston, and Jackie, and Martin
and Maya, and Oprah, and Barack
it was their fate to give birth to me
and my fate to carry their burden
a people, a black race, a juju spirit

blackness tattooed to my skin
strapped upon my back
like Sisyphus rolling it uphill

all my living breathing days
only to have it return upon me
infinitely heavier each time
shouldering the load as my mother and father did
and their parents before them did
and the generations prior to them did
all the way back to those first bodies
stolen from the shores of Africa
set on that maiden voyage to the land of the free
and the home of the cash register
futures to be determined
by auction blocks and cotton crops
yet the sun also rises my brothers, my sisters

It rises upon me
though I have known poverty so inclusive so relentless
that I walked the city streets
eyes to the ground searching for pennies
cans, bottles, plastic beverage containers
enough to buy a can of mackerel
only to return home and solve the equation
how does one divide that can six ways
as the hopeful eyes of four children
and a wife look to me, believe in me
me, so desperate that I steal
toilet paper from public restrooms
or go without, so determined that I
walk six miles to the university each day
and the same six miles home to forge
a better life for those eyes that look to me

training my mind to ignore the hunger pains
one hand strangling my stomach
to quiet the growls
that cry for more than the solitary cookie
that served as breakfast and lunch
but hopefully not dinner
the other hand darkening
the appropriate blocks of scantron sheets

clinging to the hope the sun also rises
like a life raft bobbing in an endless sea
I know it rises even though
I must sometimes beat back a deep depression
born of false starts and misgivings
failed entrepreneurship and misplaced trust
friends long escaped
and loved ones long departed

children turned adults and scattered
like dice on a crap table
to seek their own fortunes
shoulder their own burdens
while I, body withered from abuse and neglect
and the struggle that is life
look past my front porch
over vehicles now groaning from age
across property badly in need of upkeep
around a wife now resigned to the reality
upward mobility and the American dream
is more an illusion than a birthright
staring at the orange sun
like sherbert melting
above a chocolate horizon
I've been rushing toward all my life

only to realize
it is the same distance from me
as the day I was pushed
from my mother's dark womb
into a world of darker prospects
Still, I believe the sun also rises
each time tomorrow arrives holding possibilities
a child smiles into a camera
a bride slips into her wedding gown
a graduate tosses his cap into the air
the beloved falls into the embrace of her lover
a merchant hangs an open sign in the window
a woman shatters the glass ceiling

into a million fragments
a train pulls out of the station
or a ship slides safely away from harbor

a plane takes off swiftly from one airport
to set down gently at another
a teacher smiles at the bright faces
of a classroom of eager young students
an elderly couple wakes to another day
a hand drops a vote into a ballot box
the lights go down in a theatre as
a director's vision roars to life
on a giant screen
the uncertainty of night
yields itself to the promise of a new day
in which my granddaughter
places her tiny hand in mine
and ask why the sun rises
and I answer
"to bring us hope in the midst of despair."

Johnnie

Johnnie been a junkie six years runnin'
everybody run when they see him comin'
hole in his soul no man can feel it
turn your back a second Johnnie steal it

livin' in a burnt shack
hustlin' for some more crack
suckin' on a tic tac
skinny as a thumb tack
go to see his contact
with a bag of nicknacks
man say hey
if you got no money get back
Johnnie start to bargain
habit got him crawlin'
man don't move
cause he know Johnnie stallin'
push him in the chest say
cut out all yo bawlin'
ain't got no money then
don't come callin'

Johnnie been a junkie six years runnin'
everybody run when they see him comin'
hole in his soul no man can feel it
turn your back a second Johnnie steal it

Go to see his parents
steal another nicknack
say they got no money so
Johnnie say he be back
momma start to bargain
guilt got her crawlin'
poppa don't move
cause he know Johnnie stallin'
push him in the chest say
cut out all your lyin'

you don't have a job
cause you ain't been tryin'

Johnnie been a junkie six years runnin'
everybody run when they see him comin'
hole in his soul no man can feel it
turn your back a second Johnnie steal it
Sally had a gun but
now she can't find it
look out the window
see Johnnie runnin'
go to see his contact
gun in his back pack
Johnnie pull it out say
tell me where the money at
man start to bargain
tears start fallin'
Johnnie don't move
cause he know the man stallin'
push him in the chest say
cut out all yo cryin'
gun say clap clap
man start dyin'

Johnnie been a junkie six years runnin'
everybody run when they see him comin'
hole in his soul no man can feel it
anything move now Johnnie kill it.

I Hear You Talkin'

Always depending on the powers that be
living off welfare and government cheese
sending your children to inferior schools
wonder why they run around actin' a fool
talk of how you coulda been shoulda been
and if not for bad breaks you woulda been
say a prayer every now and then
glance to see if i'm buyin' in

I Hear You Talkin' but it's deeper than that
I hear you talkin' but it's deeper than that
I hear you talkin' but it's deeper than that
it's deeper than that, it's deeper than that

Buyin' magic pills and get rich schemes
payin' psychics to interpret your dreams
use lotto numbers and hormone creams
to replace the King of Kings
sayin' how your old man beat you up
but now life should be lookin' up
cause you and this new dude's hookin' up
and ain't life all about gettin' enough?

I Hear You Talkin' but it's deeper than that
I hear you talkin' but it's deeper than that
I hear you talkin' but it's deeper than that
it's deeper than that, it's deeper than that

Hoppin' round like intellectual flees
trustin' in research and Phd.s
turnin' your nose up at superstition
while dying of spiritual malnutrition
basing your life on big bang theories
thinking life's a discovery series
believing men evolved from monkeys
highminded as scientific junkies

I Hear You Talkin' but it's deeper than that
I hear you talkin' but it's deeper than that
I hear you talkin' but it's deeper than that
it's deeper than that, it's deeper than that

Rags to riches that's your story
a poster child for fame and glory
an entourage of A-List friends
Bentleys, Porches and Mercedes Benz
close to being a billionaire
penthouse bigger than a country fair
everyone envies the life you lead
you ask what else could you possibly need?

I Hear You Talkin' but it's deeper than that
I hear you talkin' but it's deeper than that
I hear you talkin' but it's deeper than that
it's deeper than that, it's deeper than that

All my life I was stumblin'
at my circumstances grumblin'
while my self esteem kept tumblin'
my soul denying the rumblin'
making mountains out of molehills
seeing mountains where there was no hills
until the Creator made me look
and find the answers in His book

Why depend on man and his seed
when God shall supply my every need
how can you trust in merchandise
and ignore the creator of life
don't know where your information's from
but I recommend Genesis chapter one
careful taking credit for your lofty place
those who exalt themselves will be abased

and one more thing before we settle the score
how come monkeys don't turn into men no more?

I Hear You Talkin' but it's deeper than that
I hear you talkin' but it's deeper than that
I hear you talkin' but it's deeper than that
it's deeper than that, it's deeper than that.

Daddy Git Cha Gun

Daddy git cha gun
and load up
cause baby girl
she done growed up
and that flat lil chest
done swolled up
and them bad lil boys
done showed up

just the other day
saw her walkin'
her and that bad lil boy
was talkin'
like a lion
he was stalkin'
even tried to kiss her
with the neighbors gawkin'

she forgot
what you taught her
see the lil necklace
he done bought her
she don't even dress
like yo' daughter
showin' more skin
than a good girl oughta

So daddy git cha, daddy git cha, daddy git cha
daddy git cha gun

Use to come straight home
like you told her
but now that
she's gotten older
it don't matter how much
you scold her
she still let that boy

put his arm round her shoulder

been wearin'
momma's perfume
paintin' her face up
like a cartoon
she growin' up
way too soon
next thing you know
that boy be up in her bedroom

please baby girl
take your time
boys only got
one thang on they mind
she says daddy
I'll be fine
but you runnin'
out of time

So daddy git cha, daddy git cha, daddy git cha
daddy git cha gun.

My Life

My life, my life, my life's
been so amazing
my life, my life, my life's
been filled with blessings
my life, my life, my life's
an open book so
welcome to my life
welcome to my life

I was a weak little ghetto kid
with wobbly knees
had asthma so bad
I could hardly breathe
had a doctor tell my mother
lady take it from me
not a day of sports glory
will your son ever see
but my grandmother prayed
for my strength and health
and a few years later
I surprised myself
on the athletic field
I straight amazed 'em
made the crowds so electric
it was like I tazed 'em
I could shake 'em down in football
hit 'em out in baseball
fly like a bird
and make magic with the roundball

Heard songs I wrote
on the radio
received awards from mayors
and been on TV shows
as a journalist met stars
and celebrities
wrote their stories for the papers

and the magazines
never had lots of money
or many diamond rings
just my share of beautiful women
and some pretty young things
went to college got some knowledge
and from merciful God
received Solomon's wisdom
to help me beat the odds
had a gun put to my head
and this dude call me nigah
still I feel blessed
cause he didn't pull the trigger
knee high to grasshoppers
way back in the day
saw the world's greatest bands
on the concert stage
Led Zeppelin, Bob Marley, Marvin Gaye
Earth, Wind & Fire, and Michael J
Springsteen, O'Jays
and Return To Forever
the list goes on forever
no music will ever be better
now I'm rockin' Jay-Z
and Alicia Keys
got that T.I. and Fifty
knockin' leaves off the trees
their rise to success
is inspiring to me
thank Beyonce'
for givin' brothers
somethin' to see

Seen days of hunger
and nights so frightening
pistols poppin'
bullets streakin'
through the hood like lightning
if they made my life a movie

they could surely sell it
cause I've been through it all
and I lived to tell it
always had big dreams
now they even bigger
and I haven't peaked yet
far as I can figure
if my words someday
bring me wealth and fame
make my lovers and the haters
all remember my name
let those who know me
certify one thang
through the joy and the madness
I've never changed
thank God for the kinda man
I became
cause all the poverty and anger
could have drove me insane
now I teach what I've learned
to those who have so much less
give them tools they can use
to discover success
taught students in school
and inmates in prisons
shared how Christ died
and told 'em how now he's risen
I've been blessed with the best
lovers, friends, and mentors
felt the warmth of God's touch
through a lifetime of winters
my story's still unfolding
though the future is hidden
sure like to know the ending
but it's still being written

My life, my life, my life's
been so amazing
my life, my life, my life's

been filled with blessings
my life, my life, my life's
an open book so
welcome to my life
welcome to my life.

Are You Still Standing

You made a vow to love and cherish
and honor each other until you perish
through sickness and health for better or worse
she promised to cling to you and you to her
but the years have come and gone
the days are hard and the nights are long
now you and the secretary are all alone
and the temptation is strong
are you still...

Never thought you'd be without someone else
but you're raising two children by yourself
you strive to teach them right from wrong
though self respect is the only thing you own
and the hustler all your neighbors talk about
has made an offer to help you out
the rent is unpaid and the bills are due
so baby girl what you gonna do?
are you still...

You took an oath to protect and serve
but the street won't give the respect you deserve
your life's on the line for those who wouldn't bother
the badge you wear represents integrity and honor
but tonight frustrations are boiling over
feels like the whole world is on your shoulders
a teenager is giving you more than you can stand
and your gun is in your hand
are you still...

The call comes in apartment house burning
as you pull on your gear your stomach's churning
your engine arrives to find the fire raging
and inside the building a child is crying
the structure will collapse before long
and you have a wife and children of your own
you think about them growing up without you

but you pledged to bear the burdens placed upon you
are you still...

Through the crowd you can plainly see
the twisted metal and scattered debris
a desperate family in need of help
rush to their aid or wait for someone else?
fear of lawsuits tell you to stay clear
the Hippocratic oath is ringing in your ears
in the midst of confusion here's your moment of truth
with those gifted hands what will you do?
are you still...

You wept and cried on bended knees
and begged the Lord to hear your pleas
to deliver you from your lifelong addiction
and if he did you'd serve him with conviction
now you search but can't find a job
and to eat you're forced to steal and rob
do you still believe God is able
with that needle on the table
are you still...

You live to protect the country you love
to honor family, Nation, and God above
you're under fire in the battle zone
a long way from family and home
your brother soldier has fallen in battle
and lay beneath death's growing shadow
the vow you made is "no one left behind"
before you face the enemy one last time
are you still...

The world will try to turn you around
life will try to wear you down
and people will plot to tear you down
but the only question that matters in the end is
Are you still standing for what you believe in?
...so are you still!

Undefined

What is it that drives me
like the engine of some machine
meets me the moment i awake
stays with me til i fall asleep
guides every step i take
forms every breath i breathe
inhabits my solitary thoughts
colors every sight i see
in a crowded room makes me lonely
keeps me forever striving for
makes me want to live without it
leaves me always wanting more
turns me from my destination
points me toward the great unknown
leads me deep into the darkness
shines a light that brings me home

I hear it in the churning waves
that beat against distant shores
i see it on the face of strangers
and in the mirror on my wall
i feel it when rays of sun
plant warm kisses on my cheek
i feel it in the chilling cold
with blankets piled head to feet
i drink it in water that quenches
thirsty simmering summer days
i've exhaled it in the mist
of freezing winters gone away
it sits beside me when i pause
on the bench beneath the trees
it lays atop me while i wait
for the night to bring me sleep

The years they come and they go
and yet somehow it remains
it sets me free to chase the future

anchors me to the past like chains
it makes me ever optimistic
things will work out for the best
it clouds my mind with depression
fills my heart with emptiness
it is the fear i must conquer
it is the love i must possess
the hand i hope will someday touch me
the voice that screams in quietness
in its presence i am speechless
i am putty in its hands
with it all the world is heaven
by it i am forever damned.

Under The Spell

Beneath the warming glow
of the giant crystal ball
waiting for the countdown
staring up with hope, desperation, faith
fingers crossed, crosses around necks
lives crossed and twisted and twisting
intersecting and dissecting
conversing and converging
diverse and divergent
but all emerging with unbridled optimism
for and in the upcoming year
about to be birthed
the divorce' looking for a new start
a new love
the praying mother waiting for the new year
to bring her wandering daughter home
the welfare mother wishing for a miracle
to keep her gas from being turned off
the newlyweds believing the new year
will be the first of a lifetime of happiness
the corporate CEO preparing to make
the hard decision of whether to lay off
3000 or 5000 employees to save his company
the teacher searching for a way to engage
a room full of inner city students
who have lost their love for life and learning
the pastor waiting for words that can inspire
his impoverished congregation
next to him the affluent pastor
inwardly begging forgiveness
for the lust that is threatening to consume
him, his marriage, and his church
the centenarian thankful to see another year
next to the woman with the newborn
whose eyes are witnessing the birth
of its first new year
the foreign exchange student caught up

in the freedom and exuberance of the moment
the unsuspecting single mother of five
who does not know that even now
the cancer that will make this new year her last
is eating its way through her body
the teenage boy and his girlfriend
who will both soon capture their dreams
of becoming professional athletes
though their love will not survive the upcoming year
the impassioned terrorist
who embraces the revelry around him
while at the same time plotting to destroy it
two strangers who will become lovers
and then strangers again
a boy lost in the sadness and anxiety
that is his life
and the mentor who will help him find
meaning and a staggering success
that will lift his family and his community
out of the abyss of hopelessness
and provide them with new jobs and new lives
a million lives soon to be affected and infected
with whatever the new year is about to bring
and another billion sets of eyes worldwide
looking up excitedly, expectantly
under the spell of the crystal ball
peering into it, believing in the power of it
for a new start, for better times, for greater faith
for health, and wealth, and forgiveness
their hopes rising as it descends
10...9... 8... 7... 6... 5... 4... 3... 2...
and the magic begins.

The Mack

I'm sitting in the corner
little Jack Horner
at my favorite cafe
planning out my day
yeh, you know the one
where the girlies come
and think they might be
seen sippin' ice tea
by Hollywood producers
those casting couch seducers
when suddenly I pause
cause in through the doors
in slow motion you walk in
pan the room and then
get seated at a table
I'm checkin' out your label
before you're even served
I work up the nerve
to walk across the room
like a camera I zoom
you don't know me
and I don't know you
but girl I think you are
the one I'm searching for
I'm standing here before you
to tell you I adore you
you may think I'm crazy
but I think you may be
that special girl I've seen
runnin' through my dreams
every night I see you
asking me to free you
from this world that has you trapped
let me take you back
come away with me

Got tickets to a show
if you'd like to go
we can sneak away
catch a matinee
if you feel my vibe
we can take a drive
cruise up the coast
to a spot I know
watch the sunset
maybe get wet
huddle in a blanket
share what we been thinkin'
before we take it further
get to know each other
even the best of lovers
started out as friends
this is the day you prayed for
the day we both were made for
I know you've been wanting
but never really tasting
the sweet life you dream of
the embrace of true love
the men in your past
could never make it last
they don't know the secrets of
how to make slow love
they never take their time
but my love is refined
I'll satisfy your body
and satisfy your mind
I don't want to scare you
but I'm here to save you
from this life of madness
wipe away your sadness
just place your heart in mine
come away with me

I know that you were mine
in another place and time

girl I swear I knew you
then somehow I lost you
I've journeyed through the ages
baby just to say this
now that I've found you
placed my arms around you
I'll be your strong soldier
shield you from the colder
let me be your nectar
provider and protector
give you every good thing
let you want for nothing
lift you into my arms
hold you above the storms
trust in what I say
girl let's run away
set out now to find
that love we left behind
leave this world so blind
for another place and time
when you were my queen
fulfillment of my dreams
and I was your pharaoh
ruler of your heart and hero
when we walked hand in hand
across the burning sands
laid in each other's arms
made love beneath the stars
if you let me in
it will be that way again
and this time I promise
it will never end
come away with me.

Your head spinnin' counterclockwise
you see eternity in my eyes
I rub my hand across your thighs
in search of a sweet surprise
I kiss you on your waiting neck

you pause a moment to catch your breath
excuse yourself for a restroom break
and while you're gone I pause to take
a glance at what's coming in the door
she's fine as you and so much more
I rise and stroll over to her table
sit down and slowly check her label
come away with me I begin...

Gone In An Instant

In all his life he'd never seen a bride
more beautiful
when they arrived at the dock the weather
was wonderful
that special night he held her close and spoke
of their future together
before they said goodnight they promised to
love each other ever and ever

with a jolt they awoke
put on robes opened the door
people spoke in hushed voices
confused they waited an hour more
they kissed goodbye to hide his tears
he turned his face to the chilling breeze
from a lifeboat she watched the ship
disappear into the silent sea

gone in an instant

For thirty years or more this house has been
their only home
now they're being told to evacuate and leave it
to the storm
but a man doesn't work all his life just to
throw it all away
when he refused to leave she knew in her heart
she had to stay

The winds blew sky turned black
the rain came the river rose
thunder roared lightning cracked
streets flooded the levee broke
the house swamped the attic filled
huddled together water rushing in
from his arms she is torn
he reaches out for her and then

gone in an instant

Woke to see the sparkle that lives in
your laughing eyes
greeting each morning like you're waking for
the very first time
you pack our lunches I assist with kisses
upon your lovely face
before you rush out the door we turn to share
one last embrace

they say you pulled onto
the freeway and a tire blew
the car spun horns blared
the diesel braked the driver knew
the life we built love we felt
if I had known it was our last embrace
I would've held onto you could've held onto you
should've held onto you...

gone in an instant
gone in an instant
gone in an instant.

Chapter Three:
Hot, Steamy, Sexy

License my roving hands, and let them go,
Before, behind, between, above, below.

John Donne

Tell Me How You Want It

We can start by laying down
on a luxurious sheep skin rug
in front of the dancing flames
of the crackling fireplace
I can begin at the nape of your neck
and work my kisses
down your voluptuous length
to that secret place
move my warm hands
around your waist
across your stomach
and down your thighs
pull you close
and make the sweetest love
slowly kissing your mouth
while seeing my passion
reflected in your eyes

We can hide in the seclusion
of my back yard paradise
beside the sparkling waters
of the swimming pool
as I lotion you down
beneath the soothing sun
serve you cold beverages and fruit
like the rich and famous do
massage your feet
your calves and thighs
your neck and back
until you're supple and loose
suckle your tongue with mine
until the juices
drip from our lips
thick and sweet as a honeydew
shed our towels
slide into the heated pool
and while you grip the side

come in from behind my honey
and make you feel as real
as brand new money

How you want it girl
tell me how you want it
how you want it
tell me how you want it baby
how you want it now
tell me how you want it
cause I'll give it to you
any way you want it girl

I can pull back the drapes
and show you a million lights
from the heights of my hillside retreat
on this night so beautiful
and we can make love
with the moon above
bathing us in silky white
fluorescent glow
we can go old school
do it nice and slow
with Luther and Teddy P
serenading us in stereo
as I stoke your fire
with tongue flicks and licks
until my name is
the only word on your lips
I can guide you beneath me
and pound out a savage rhythm
til you surrender to the awesome power
generated by my mighty hips

We can sit down by candlelight
white table cloth and fine china
sip wine from crystal goblets
eat a feast so good it's magical
then clear the table

climb on top and quench our appetites
while the surround sound
plays smooth jazz or classical
then we can take a drive
to this private spot atop the mountain
and just talk for hours
you sharing your secrets me sharing mine
climb into the preheated back seat
of my spacious Maybach 57
make love like anxious teenagers
enjoying our bodies for the first time
then drive to the ocean
where I'll place around your neck
a token of my devotion my queen
and you and me
can watch the orange sherbet sun
melt into the glistening sea

So, how you want it girl
tell me how you want it
how you want it now
tell me how you want it baby
how you want it
please tell me how you want it
cause you know you can get it
any way you want it girl.

We Woke Up On Fire

(for all those still in love)

We woke up on fire
we woke up on fire
we woke up on fire
burning with desire

Hey... Can I rub it all down from front to back
shine it up like an apple on a grocery rack
tuck it into my pocket when I say goodnight
shoot it off like a rocket in the morning light
wanna yank it, shank it, turn it round and spank it
put it in a glass and I might even drank it
swing it like a flag from side to side
hitch it up like a wagon and take a ride
so elastic, just like plastic, I believe it's, so fantastic
stay with me girl til the end of days
I'm so in love let me count the ways

We woke up on fire
we woke up on fire
we woke up on fire
burning with desire

Wanna ride it like an indian bareback
gonna stick it to you girl like a thumb tack
make it yell like a cowboy yeehah!
let it sing like a plowboy eeyah!
wanna see it, free it wish that I could be it
wine and dine and chicken fricassee it
fly through the air like a loopty loop
let me jump through it girl like a hoopty hoop
stop your chasin' girl you got me
falling for you try and stop me
never ever gonna go home again
might as well open up and let me in

We woke up on fire
 we woke up on fire
 we woke up on fire
 burning with desire

Let me bounce it like a baby on my knee
make it rise and fall like a stormy sea
spread it out like stars in a midnight sky
heat it up little girl like a pizza pie
left side, right side, inside, outside
lovely view from every side
cream of the crop no need to test
send the rest of 'em home girl you're the best
bop it, pop it, lift and drop it
never felt anything like it
time out girl let me catch my breath
let my tombstone read "he was loved to death."

We woke up on fire
 we woke up on fire
 we woke up on fire
 your name should be Desire.

Let's Get Lost

Girl I got a confession to make
don't know how much more I can take
got me so wired up I got the shakes
got my back so tired it's about to break
every time I think we've reached the peak
you show me another plateau to reach
the moment our love looks horizontal
girl you take it on up to another level

when our bodies get to knockin'
and the bed starts to rockin'
ain't no way I'm stoppin'
once I get that body poppin'

love the way your body moves
when we're front to back
when i slip into that groove
we're like torch and match
all through the day
you're so nice and sweet
then you turn into a wildcat
between the sheets

Uh oh
i feel my hand start to creep
I know
it's late and I should let you sleep
maybe baby just one more time
before lights off
and we say goodnight

I think about you all day while I work
heart starts jumpin' round inside my shirt
my head starts filling with fantasies
of the things I'd do if you were next to me

we could do it on my desk
like business professionals
I can be your priest
do it in the confessional
do it on a float
during the Rose Bowl processional
do it in the forest
it would feel so natural
 Tarzan and Jane wit it
so wild when we get it
scream so loud
wake the whole damn village!

only takes one time
to make me confess
when it comes to makin' love
girl you're the best
who'd have thought a shy girl
in a cotton dress
would be off the charts
with sexiness
wanna turn you loose
but I cain't move
stuck to you girl
like a new tatoo
wanna make love to you
baby 9 to 5
and still be available
for overtime

Yo, clock me in for somma that?

all down the block
they can hear our bodies echo
even got the neighbors
tryin' to look into our windows
save some for later
I keep tellin' myself
but when you back it up like a truck

girl I gotta ugh, ugh

I try to ignore you
just to calm me down
but you get out on the floor
and you break me down
when you do that little dance step
wanna make romance step
slide to the side
and you add that little two step
turn in slow circles baby
round and round
then you work that sensual belly dance
up and down
I try to fight the feelin'
but you're eyes say come and get it
even though I'm tryin' to quit it
girl you know I gotta hit it

Just
one time gotta hit that G-spot
serve it
to me while it's still hot
git it til your lips cry baby please
get your hips vibrating from those multiple OGs

Uh no
it's time for me to go to work
can we
do it while I iron my shirt
promise not to burn it if we do
unless baby girl you want me to

baby let me up that's enough
got me runnin' late
know you want it girl
but it's 8 so you gotta wait
no no baby, baby please
don't show me that

time to hit the flo' gotta go
where's my coat and hat
Ooh now baby
you've gone and done it
might as well lay back
and tell me how you want it
now tell me how you want it girl
just the way you want it girl
how you want it when you want it
cause I want it like you want it

Uh oh
I think I just hit the spot
cause you
yellin' baby please don't stop
squeezin' me like a boa constrictor
shoutin' my name every damn time I lick ya

you talk so dirty
but it sounds so clean
my imagination's spinnin'
like a washing machine
Gotta call in sick
third time this week
I'm a strong black brotha
but for you I'm weak
the refrigerator's stocked
plenty food to eat
so baby let's get lost in between these sheets

Uh Oh, uh oh
I know, I know
here we go, here we go, here we go
Whew!!!

She Like The Way

She like the way
i scramble her eggs
she like the way
i massage her legs
she like the way
i chauffeur her round town
she like the way
i lotion her down
she like the way
i fix her internet
she like the way
i make her body wet
she like the way
i send flowers just because
she like the way
i express my deepest love

She like the way i do it when we do it
the way i get all up into it
make it vibrate to the core
make it beg and cry for more
make it open like a rose
wrap around me then tightly close
make it want me night and day
yeah, uh-huh, she like the way

She like the way
i repaired her fence post
she like the way
i send her love notes
she like the way
i open doors like a gentleman
she like the way
my muscles feel while cuddling
she like the way

my butt looks when i walk
she like the way
i make her body talk
she like the way
my voice sounds deep and low
she like the way
i make love nice and slow

She like the way i dance when we dance
make her feel like makin' romance
when i place my hand on her hips
guide her to me and kiss her soft lips
pause a moment to admire her sexiness
then move in close until we breast to chest
whisper things that take her breath away
yeah, oh yeah, she like the way

She like the way
i play basketball
she like the way
i never forget to call
she like the way
i take her out to dinner
she like the way
i feel when i'm in her
she like the way
i play her piano
she like the way
i light incense and candles
she like the way
i make her feel like a woman
she like the way
my flow keeps her comin'

She like the way i tell her when i tell her
come rain or shine we'll always be together

holding hands everywhere we go
i'm not afraid to let the whole world know
i've found someone who is more than special
on my heart i've carved her initials
she knows i place no one above her
but most of all she like the way i love her

yeah, i know, she like the way...

Waterbead

I awoke this morning thinking of you
my eyes popped open
and I immediately sprung to attention
my body humming and tingling
at the very thought of you
it is barely dawn and i've been up all night
far too early for me to relinquish sleep
but it is impossible to push you
out of my head
images of your magnificent frame
nudge me into consciousness
pulling my mind back to last night
again enticing me from bed
across the room to your favorite chair
where you tie me up and tie me down
then with my hands unable to grasp
your voluptuous curves
you fall upon my neck
like a blood starved vampire
biting into it and sucking it dry
before climbing onto my lap
steadying and impaling yourself
driving your hips forward into me
slow and methodically
then as time urges you on
increasing the pace and intensity
ignoring my agonized groans
and my helpless hands
unable to control you
you pound yourself into me
pound me into you with a fury
biting down on your bottom lip
a look of wild-eyed urgency
on your face

Not able to spank your bottom
or guide and manipulate your rhythm

like i usually do
all I can do is throw my head back
watch you and feel you
as you chase ecstasy
finally overtaking it
engulfing it, consuming it
like a fiery feast deep in your pelvis
squeezing it until it explodes
sending shock waves of pleasure
rocketing and scattering through you
spilling out of you in uncensored shrieks
and percolating fluids
the visceral fireworks igniting you
then boomeranging back upon me
grabbing me by the throat
and forcing out guttural groans
my chest heaving and body surrendering
to the flood, the rush
of pleasure streaking through me
like a train of desire
as you collapse against my shoulder
both of us gasping

When the vision finally releases me
I drag myself into the shower
closing myself in and turning the handles
until the spray of the water
is hot and forceful as I can stand it
closing my eyes
I let the water blast me into submission
causing every tense muscle to relax
as I exhale and open my eyes
I become aware of a mysterious sensation
with water hurling itself against me
in one unified powerful thrust
I feel one solitary waterbead
set itself apart from the flow
dripping from the tips of my hair
down onto my forehead

circling my eye and running down
across my cheekbone
rolling like a marble down my face
trickling past the stubble on my cheek
pausing momentarily
at the corner of my lips
then continuing to my chin
before leaping onto my chest
weaving through the slickened hair
over the mound of my pectoral muscle
mesmerized by its individuality
I trap it with my bicep
and attempt to redirect it
with my fingertips
but it springs onto my stomach
and skateboards over my abdominals
staggering slightly in between
each hardened tube
I turn in a half circle
and watch it circle around to my glutes
entering the canyon that separates them
and exiting the other end
then defying gravity it circles me again
and swims upstream like a salmon
until it reaches my lower stomach
then zigzags its way
through the hairs covering my groin
pausing to gaze at what it sees there
gliding onto and playfully inspecting me
before sliding down the length of me
and dripping from the tip onto my thigh
navigating over the rise of my thigh
it races down and around to my calf
goes barreling over it
and streaks down to my ankle
before bouncing onto my foot
where it sits sparkling
saying one last goodbye
before jumping onto the tile floor

and swirling around the vortex
that escorts it down the drain

Now creatively inspired I shut off the water
with intentions of retrieving my pen
I open the shower door
and reach through the mist for my towel
but to my surprise
what I grasp is your hand
pushing the water from my eyes
I see you standing naked before me
a look of wild-eyed urgency on your face
hot, steamy, sexy
you step into the shower
and close the door behind you.

The Tempest

With angry words
I have driven you to bed
regretting now
every wayward thing I said
into your doorway
I silently creep
pausing a moment
just to watch you gently sleep
I kneel to wake you
with the kiss I hope will please
you wake to find
I am down on bended knees
I take your hand
and place it to my chest
where the trembling rhythm
ask forgiveness
and without words
for words can be untrue
know every beat of my heart
beats for you only

I know, I know, I know, I know
like the tempest I sometimes blow
across your calm and peaceful sea
blackened skies so threatening
causing tidal waves to rise
and toss us both from side to side
but quickly as the storm was here
just as quickly it disappears

And now I've come
to make it up to you
I am your servant
tell me what to do
like tears from heaven
I made your teardrops fall
now with my kisses

let me gently dry them all
you are my queen
let me bow down at your feet
work my way up
to where the honey's oh so sweet
if I have hurt you
any of 365 days
let me make love to you
in 365 ways
all through the night
let me again regain your trust
refuse me not
for make love to you I must

I know, I know, I know, I know
like the tempest I sometimes blow
across your ocean calm and bright
turning your morning into night
if ever you look into my eyes
and see the tempest on the rise
fear not my love for I am here
to make the tempest disappear

The icy words
that drove you to retreat
let our passion
now melt with twice the heat
and in their place
let me speak sweet words of bliss
and with my tongue
start a fire in your midst
tear down walls
pain has caused you to erect
around the heart
I will never again neglect
forgiving queen
take my apology under cover
don't turn away
for I will have no other lover

hold me inside you
til the sun is on the rise
and ecstasy
are the stars that light your eyes

I know, I know, I know, I know
the tempest scares you when it blows
causing tears like rain to fall
but now my love I've dried them all
if ever the tempest reappears
fear not my love for I am here
and all the tempest can really do
is draw my heart closer to you.

Nice 'N' Easy

I hear your key turn in the door
I hear your footsteps on the floor
Friday night no work tomorrow
time to chase away all our sorrows
tell me baby how was your day
I'll take your jacket and put it away
here's a cold glass of Chardonnay
While I massage your stress away

I got a hot bath waitin' for you
dinner be ready in an hour or two
left work early canceled my plans
to get ready to fulfill your demands
let me help you out of those clothes
baby slip into your favorite robe
one button, two button, three button, four
shake it loose and let it slide to the floor

Follow me girl down the hall
pause for kisses against the wall
under the bubbles you can gently fall
I'll let you soak til I hear your call
I wash you down from head to toe
dry you off baby nice and slow
take you to bed where the stereo
is busy playing all your favorite songs

Now it's time we get into it
don't have to ask girl you know how we do it
every movement nice and fluid
you know I'm gonna get those juices brewin'
You say
Ooh baby, you know how to please me
I love when you do it nice 'n' easy
work it baby til it's just right
don't even have to go to sleep tonight

I can tell by the look on your face
the time has come to quicken the pace
I kiss your neck and lock you in place
it's time to take you to that heavenly space
boom boom jiggy jiggy boom boom
the sound of our bodies echo through the room
boom boom jiggy jiggy boom boom
got you moanin' and groanin' and singin' a tune

Feelin' good from head to feet
we makin' love and the lovin' is sweet
cain't go to Vegas cause the budget is tight
but we can take a trip to paradise
when the pleasure's got you goin' insane
I love to hear you baby callin' my name
the room is soundproof go 'head and scream
I got the cure for your every pain

I know somewhere deep in the night
when the tremors of love subside
I wouldn't trade in a billion lives
the way you make me feel inside
Ooh baby, you know how to please me
I love when you do it nice 'n' easy
take a moment to recover your stride
cause ain't nobody gonna sleep tonight

Boom boom jiggy jiggy boom boom
boom boom jiggy jiggy boom boom
boom boom jiggy jiggy boom boom
boom boom jiggy jiggy boom boom.

Spiritual Love

I'll never forget
how the first time I touched you
your whole body trembled
there were tears in your eyes
you wanted it to be so right
it took hours for the flames to kindle
and when I started to love you
you thought I had drugged you
the room was spinnin' and your head so light
and when you thought it was over
I just rolled you over
and we made love all through the night
and in the mornin' you wondered
where I found the thunder
that made lightning race through your veins
you were so satisfied
I could tell by your eyes
you wanted me in your life to stay

Cause there's an anointing in my hands
when you're under my command
that heals every hurt you've ever felt
and a fire in my kiss
once I touch your lips
that makes your every sad memory melt
and the peace in my arms
lets you slip into a place
where no worry or harm can reach you
it's not just physical love we makin'
it's a gift from above
this is Spiritual Love

When I make love to you
no need to tell me what to do
before you think it I'm already there
no need to address
where to touch you next

just moan cause I'm touching you there
don't even have to speak
our bodies are so in synch
the rhythm's always just how you want it
you can just let me drive
girl lay back and ride
and we'll arrive at the exact place you wanted

There's an anointing in my hands
when you're under my command
that heals every hurt you've ever felt
and a fire in my kiss
once I touch your lips
that makes your every sad memory melt
and the peace in my arms
lets you slip into a place
where no worry or harm can reach you
it's not just physical love
it's a divine gift from above
my queen we makin' Spiritual Love

And now you know
when my voice gets low
the kind of ecstasy I have in store
that's why you get so excited
when I dim the lights
turn off the phones and lock the doors
when our room becomes the world
and the world becomes this room
and this room becomes our paradise
girl it's just you and I
under a crystal blue sky
feeding our appetites
when our eyes meet
it's like a symphony
I the musician and you the instrument
when I stroke and caress you
the beautiful sounds you release
make our masterpiece so evident

these sensual ballads we wake
no one else can create
because no lyrics or notes can convey it
though others desperately try
this composition we write
baby only you and I can play it

Cause there's an anointing in my hands
when you're under my command
that heals every hurt you've ever felt
and a fire in my kiss
once I touch your lips
that makes your every sad memory melt
and the peace in my arms
lets you slip into a place
where no worry or harm can reach you
it's not just physical love
it's a divine gift from above
girl this is Spiritual Love.

Strokin'

From the first kiss it was like a dance
a never ending storybook romance
friends said it couldn't last much longer
through the years it's only gotten stronger
when we're alone with the doors locked tight
the curtains drawn and we dim those lights
your beauty shines like a Hollywood movie queen
transports like a long black limousine
into a world of pure sensuality
my body yearns for what you gonna do to me
even more erotic than what you can do
are the steamy things i'm gonna do to you
makin' sweet love under the skylight
where the glow of the stars shine so bright
we start strokin' bathed in moonlight
and end just a little after sunrise

If i make you scream it's all in the game
every night of pleasure cost a little bit of pain
even if we rock til the bed is broke
i'm like a Swiss watch girl i never miss a stroke

Don't rush we'll be makin' love all night
i won't stop til i know you're satisfied
even after i got you feelin' butterflies
i'll flip you over and hit it from the backside
don't be afraid to tell me how you want it baby
gonna give it to you every way you want it baby
some tongue cause i know it makes you crazy
close out with the jackhammer baby
workin' together like skis on a sky slope
love the way you get up for the downstroke
you holdin' back cause you don't wanna lose it
another stroke and you put your body to it
don't hurry we a long way from the end
i'm blessed with the stamina of ten men
your man before me made love fast

my love you can time by the hour glass

If i make you scream it's all in the game
every night of pleasure cost a little bit of pain
even if we rock til the bed is broke
i'm like a Swiss watch girl i never miss a stroke.

Knockin' Ze Boots

Been three weeks on the road without you
every spare minute thinkin' about you
and all the crazy things I'd do
the moment I'm back home with you
no more nights spent alone
alert the neighbors daddy's home
text your friends "do not disturb"
tell everyone on myspace pass the word
let your facebook girls know
you'll post pictures later
twitter your co-workers
no need to hold the elevator
mommy's getting her heater fixed
and she's gonna need those vacation days
real quick

So good to see your smiling face
but I got the fever no time to waste
how you been, ok, let the games begin'
you become the lamb chop and I'm the lion
I'm chasing you down our hallway jungle
and clothes are flyin'
stop runnin' girl it's time to rumble
you pretty quick but I put the Z in zoom
how convenient to catch you in the bedroom
I go WWF and lift you above my head
spend you round and round
aim for the bed
and gently pin you down
like you always do you start to giggle
I tickle you with my tongue
and you start to wiggle
I take out my thermometer
you say ah and I stick it in
I better get to work
you got a temperature of 110
I reach into my first aid kit for the KY jelly

rub a dub dub on the mound
just below your belly

Now I'm an olympic gymnast
dashing toward your pummel horse
I somersault throw the air
land and stick it
and to make sure you give me a 10
on the way down I lick it
now I turn jockey and you turn thoroughbred
I'm riding you like it's the Kentucky Derby
your hair blowing in the breeze
I use my hand like a riding crop
and spank your thigh just above the knees
you look back and say, one more if you would
ooh whip it daddy, whip it good
our adrenaline racing we both start sighing
you spread your legs and sparks start flying
our body heat rises from the bed
and fans out across the ceiling
setting off the sprinklers
but we can't fight the feeling
our neighbors see smoke
pouring from our bedroom window
they call the fire department and say
hey don't be amazed
but I think we got ourselves a five alarm blaze
three engines arrive
hook up their hoses
and bust through our door
the captain's eyes grow wide as he says
never seen a fire started like that before
the crew camps out around the bed
and the captain stands on a chair
he examines the sprinklers
pretending not to stare
you reach for your robe
but I spank your hand and say
lay back girl you ain't goin' nowhere

When the police department arrives
the head detective investigates the scene
he peeps through the window
and sees me gettin' away clean
he shouts mark off the area boys
they grab yellow tape and start peelin' it
they ask, what you see detective
he says
some brotha's on top of some sista killin' it
a few minutes later the news crew arrives
they set up their cameras
and start filming us live
I look at you and you look at me
then we both look at each other on HDTV
I refocus my attention on my favorite girl
as the broadcast goes out around the world
a billion Chinese are watching on satellite
as you wrap your legs around me so tight
I hear my ribs start sizzlin'
did I fail to mention we changed positions?
Charities are selling tickets to our show
to feed the needy
while a million Africans are cheering us on
in Swahili

With every stroke the world calls out for more
the bed legs are bouncing
like pogo-sticks across the floor
I forgot to put the pillow
behind the head board
so now it's flapping its jaws
smacking our freshly painted mural
knocking plaster off the walls
you feelin' so good
your body begins to levitate
but with my superior hang time
I block your escape
halfway to the ceiling you let out a moan

come on daddy drive Mrs. Daisy on home
I grab on to the ceiling fan
to gain some traction
over in Vegas they placin' bets
and laying odds on the action
we get a telegram from Norway
that says we have two Nobel Prizes coming
seems all the heat from our bodies
reversed the effects of global warming
and the middle east is finally at peace
all men embracing as brothers
cause they're too busy watching us
to keep fighting each other
finally massive orgasms
shake you to your core
Cal-Tech checks the equipment
and screams, holy mackerel 12.4

You're pounding me on my back
to withstand the bliss
I wink and whisper
what you likin' this
in three different languages you cry out
si, qui, yes
from a pub in Germany
a man raises his glass and salutes
he says
dem two yahnkees sure know how to
knock ze boots
when the last tremor hits
it releases a mushroom cloud
that spreads across the seven continents
before it disappears
Gucci bottles the vapors
cause the scent falls somewhere between
P-Diddy and Elizabeth Taylor
when we touch down on the bed
applause goes up around the planet
and some dude from NASA announces

Houston, the eagle has landed
our pit bull fires up a doobie
lookin' through our window pane
he barks
damn I've done it doggy style before
but that was off the chain!
we lay cuddled together
your head on my chest
as you whisper softly
ooh baby you still the best
the moment I kiss your forehead and say
couldn't have done it without you mama
a reporter hands me the phone and whispers
it's President Obama
I say, yes sir Mr. President
he says, boy you a credit to our nation
me and Michele just finished giving you two
a standing ovation
but could I ask you to do it one more time
the secret service forgot to put in the tape
i answer, for sure brother President
just give us ten minutes to recuperate.

Got It Bad For You

How can I even in a lifetime express
the degree to which I am blessed
to have you for my very own
to never again have to walk alone
words are either too many or too few
to accurately convey my gratitude
you are one in a trillion girl
worth more than a zillion girls
my queen I straight out adore you
my love is so deep I wanna bow before you
you are more precious than the air I breathe
you are everything a man could ever need
I got flaws and faults I'm just real wit it
but you came fully equipped to deal wit it
right here right now I tell the world it's true
I'm uniquely and completely devoted to you

When I was down you lifted me
when I am bound you set me free
when I am weak you nourish me
when I am lost you rescue me
the moment others turned and walked away
is the moment you came into my life to stay
because you refused to be afraid of me
I love the man you made of me
whenever I am disrespected
your prayers help me stay connected
when the world is full of rejection
within your arms I find protection
through raging storms to keep love afloat
you've never hesitated to pay the cost
when my burdens are too heavy
you willingly help me bear the cross

Let my love fall upon you like rain
to wash away your every pain
I'm a willing pupil teach me how to be

anything everything you will ever need
know that I can't sleep without you here
don't even wanna eat until you are near
when we are apart I'm not whole
because you are the center of my very soul
from the early moment I awake
until the late hour I fall asleep
every solitary thing I do
my love I do it all for you
you are my motivation my inspiration
my sweet sensation my fascination
timeless to you will be my dedication
rest assured my love will have no expiration

When you touch me my body quakes
when I hold you my passion wakes
when I hurt you my heart breaks
your body is my great escape
don't want you to somehow miss it
so let me make it a little more explicit
I've found forever in your eyes
find sweet release between your thighs
all it takes to make me rise
is simply for you to walk by
blood starts racing through my veins
pheromones start firing in my brain
the sight of you naked is such a high
each time we make love I thank God I'm alive
please don't think such talk is rude of me
I'm just tellin' you what you do to me

Birds are given wings to fly
fish fins to swim the sea
soldiers are given courage to try
cheetahs given legs for speed
trees given roots to grow
God gave me you because He knows
no one else in this world could be
all the things you are to me

Got it bad for you and I admit it
got it bad for you and I can't quit it
got it bad for you and it grows each day
got it bad for you and don't want it to go away
got it bad for you and no one can change it girl
got it bad for you and I'll tell the world
baby girl, baby girl, baby girl, you know it's true
I got it bad for you.

Hot, Steamy, Sexy

I was a bachelor eating pizza from paper dishes
up popped a genie who said his name was Alowicious
he said I'm here to grant you your three wishes
I asked what kind of government program this is
just three chances to create something delicious?
he said use to be four but inflation's gotten vicious
he asked, you want, cars, houses, money, large fishes
maybe something both tasty and nutritious
I asked him for some time to think it through
he said he'd return in a day or two
all night I wondered what to do
how I could have my cake and eat it too
he returned ready to make wishes come true
I said ok genie here's the three wishes I choose
hot, steamy, sexy, then alakazam and poof
first came the smoke then there was you.

Chapter Four:
Welcome to the Revolution

*Those who make peaceful revolution impossible
will make violent revolution inevitable.*

John F. Kennedy

*A revolution is not a bed of roses… a revolution
is a struggle to the death between the future
and the past.*

Fidel Castro

Disposable Nation

Don't do the crime cause you can't do the time
givin' up your prime you must be out of your mind
courts all backed up prisons got 'em stacked up
judges slingin' time like lunches all packed up
slavery's over ain't no more cotton to pick
check yourself, stop livin' by the edge of yo dick
lambs to the slaughter nigahs hustlin' for a dollar
you can lead a horse to water but you can't make him drink
fools behind bars 2 million strong
you can send a kid to school but you can't make him think
when you were in 3rd grade plans were being made
to build this steel cage and here you be
how were they so sure? They checked your reading score
the writing's on the wall but you couldn't see
genocide, fratricide, homicide, suicide
any way you slice it means extinction
don't mistake fear for respect my brother
the difference between them makes for quite a distinction
don't be misled by standing ovations
you're still a part of the disposable nation

Pick 'em up, lock 'em up, build a place to stock 'em up
charge 'em $3 for a cup of soup
pay ourselves to babysit 'em round the clock
hire public pretenders to keep 'em in the loop
walkin' the prison yard rackin' your brains
thinkin' bout how to get back in the game
blinded by bright lights lost in confusion
thinkin' you winnin' when you all the time losin'
usin' the same method wantin' different results
that's retardation homey best be changin' your thoughts
the world keeps turnin' with or without you
get locked up friends forget all about you
back on the street to catch another case
strike three! get this nigah out of my face
put him in the big house dumb nigah warehouse
make him love this house more than His house

own him never let him back on the block
keep him til he leaves inside a box
not a dime wasted on rehabilitation
another number in the disposable nation

Chester the molester's takin' care of baby Sally
while momma the crack whore's givin' head in the alley
the rich and powerful thumbing they nose
politicians playin' dumb singin' "that's the way the wind blows"
if you send our national guard to Taquit
how come they can't patrol our city streets
to put an end to this crack house fair
this methed out lair, smoked out nightmare
or is dope your solution serves your purpose
to sedate and thereby control the masses
while you milk the people dry with taxes
swingin' fear of the people on the people like battle axes
a horse after a carrot a dog chasin' the rabbit
got the country addicted to fear and panic
fear of blacks cause you might get robbed
fear of mexicans cause they'll take your job
fear of asians cause they smarter than we
fear of gays cause they HIV
fear of everyone except yourself
when there's nothing to fear but fear itself

 I'm the voice you wish would shut the fuck up
while you rape and oppress? No such luck
I'm a voice cryin' in the wilderness
the hammer of God to put an end to your madness
to smash into pieces and scatter to the wind
this voodoo hoodoo you got us bottled up in
loose your wicked devices and free my people
shout it from the jail to the steeple this shit is evil
you play with witchcraft when you cut that batch in half
like a TV sitcom you makin' me laugh
that heat you packin' can't hurt your real enemy
he walks where only spiritual eyes can see
I'm tellin' you blood we don't fight against flesh and blood

if you crippin' he ain't trippin' he's killin' the whole hood
read the holy book and you'd know this
stop lettin' the adversary to and fro this
we thuggin' our way into oblivion
the future of our race is the luggage we carryin'
don't take another hit of what you smokin'
the Apocalypse has begun and God ain't jokin'

 How can every other race get it together
and we be still under the weather
suckin' on a crack pipe, sniffin' them coke lines
believin' our own hype, drinkin' that cheap wine
desecrating urinating on the temple inside
making it another dark place to hide
if I have to turn profit so be it
anything everything to help ya'll see it
hear ye, hear ye the word of the Lord
you nigahs wastin' the gift you nigahs party too hard
wish my hand was wide as a constellation
to pimp slap this disposable nation
shake 'em up, wake 'em up, take they pipes and break 'em up
hit 'em with reality they denyin' slap slap
club 'em with truth til they cryin'
my nigahs wise up, rise up, open your eyes up
figure out the life you livin' don't add up
stand up mighty sons of pharaohs and kings
hold your head up daughters of the African queens
ascend to your rightful place in this creation
reverse the curse on this disposable nation.

Father Figure

The things he said to me
 i can never utter
Even now they cling to me
 i wear them like a sweater
This is his legacy
 always hoped I'd do better
Chaser of women neglecter of children, man
 got me tarred and feathered
I know it's killing me
 people I'm not blind to it
Thought I could beat it see
 if I put my mind to it
Years have come and gone still here I be
 I'm just resigned to it
I'm a nigah finger on the trigger
 Oh God, don't let me pull it
I try to shake it
 but it sticks to me like napalm
I try to fake it
 but I can't keep this damn mask on
If I forget it
 the mirror reminds me where I came from
I'm a victim of genetics he's inside me
 tickin' like a time bomb
How can I escape
 this headless horseman keeps chasin' me
Am I slave to the past
 and will I ever be free
This poem is proof
 he's in here haunting me
like father like son here we come
 together eternally
He's overtaking me
 i'm tired I can't sleep at night
I'm losing my sanity
 though I'm holding on with all my might
Jesus help me

it's beyond my ability to fight
I feel myself slippin' am I trippin'
 or is he my destiny
I tried chokin' him out with education
 but pain don't recognize no degree
I tried casting him out with religion
 but he's on the pew next to me
I tried smokin' him out with herbs
 still he won't let me be
He's in my veins in my brain pushing me to the edge
 how long before I'm over the ledge
As time goes by I walk like him
 must mean he's moving inside me now
I'm beginning to talk like him
 must mean we think the same thoughts now
Won't be long before I act like him
 then heaven help us all now
I got this rage in a cage help me hold him
 don't let him destroy me now
All the wrong he did
 am I condemned to repeat
How soon will I be him
 will I succumb to defeat
The distance between us is slim
 no room left to retreat
I am him he is me is this what they mean
 when they say Father Figure.

Zombieland

In the last days the evil quickens
time is short and the clock is tickin'
the water's tainted see how it sickens
the plot is hatched now see how it thickens

Dem always diagnose that you sick for sure
dem always got the pills but they got no cure
dem medicate the young so they hooked for life
might as well kill 'em with a gun or knife
dem say spank your children and you go to jail
the children no get spanked so dey raisin' hell
you take 'em to the doctor and you pay the fee
him tell you that your child got the A.D.D
dem write a prescription but what you don't know
dem makin' him a zombie under their control
dem make believe they angels but they evil man
dem making countless billions running Zombieland

Zombie boy grow to be a zombie man
like all the other zombies follow zombie plan
he no want control he just want his pills
he no have lots of money just got lots of bills
he no cast a vote so he got no voice
he do what dem say cause he got no choice
he turn to drugs try and ease his mind
can't support his habit so he turn to crime
in prison no accept responsibility
he say what you expect I got the A.D.D
your elders tried to tell you but you turned away
always want to raise your child the modern way
when we were young we no have the A.D.D
we burn our energy playin' on the street
and all we don't burn we learn to melt
or momma melt it for us with the switch and belt
But dem no care how it use to be
cause zombies make dem rich with the A.D.D.

Invincible

I am the watchman
high above the fortress wall
surveying all
seeing even the beetle
who creeps and crawls
part african prince
the jewel of God's creation
part native american
warrior from the Choctaw nation
birthed on the unforgiving streets
of South Central LA
stamped by poverty
will forged into steel
by trials and hardships
the winds of injustice
the drenching rains of hatred
baptized me with a hunger
that can never be spoken
often bent but never broken
my mind created to strive
my hands formed to fight
called forth to lead my people
out of darkness into the marvelous light
wielding words like a knife
that cuts through the bone
and deep into the marrow
untouchable to those who seek to corrupt
unmovable by the forces that deconstruct
unbreakable to those that cause division
incapable of aborting the mission

A ninja in your midst
striking at the heart of fear
then disappearing into the mist
a prophet, a warrior, a deliverer
sprung forth from the slaves womb
to deliver her

able to slide through cracks
in your cerebral wall
to deliver you from all
that would cause you to fall
a slave to none
thus feared by all
who bring men under submission
through lies and derision
the mental circumcision
my blood pure, hands sure, back strong
mind built to endure
the minutes, hours, days
in silent repose
then suddenly I explode
waging war on those
who seek to depose
my cherished tribe, my people
thrusting my sword of truth
into their hearts of evil
overturning the tables
chasing the money mongers
from the temple
plain and simple
those who are not with me
are against me
and those who do not gather scatter
to break your choke hold on my people
your backbone I will shatter
smash your grinding wheel into pieces
toss it to the wind
before my life's at end
I will slaughter them
by thousands even millions
gather my army like Sicilians
mold warriors out of ordinary civilians
liberate my people by the billions, Rah!

I will carve the word freedom
upon their chest

bankrupt those who invest
in the genocide, homicide, fratricide
of my sisters and brothers
those who destroy the minds of our children
to steal them from their mothers
seduce our fathers
with wine, women, and song
teach my brother my sister to steal
then lock them in cages
their whole life long
make them imitations of human beings
then judge them for their wrongs
as though you are not
the father of their actions
having stripped them of their heritage
and divided them into fractions
in the prime of their youth
turned them from the truth
toward myths and fables
chasing what does not exist
til they are no longer able
to win first place in your crooked race
you grind their dreams into paste
their names forever erased

But now enters the ninja
I am the avenger
of the displaced and dispossessed
come to arrest all
who will not willingly surrender
divest themselves of their bloodstained
legal tender
for your evil deeds
I will cause you to remember
I will rape the rapist
leave him to wallow in his shame
beat the con man at his own game
strip naked the corporate thieves
bring the greedy to their knees

and none can bribe or appease
for I am above the reproach of these
who lubricate their lies
with fire water and chemical highs
their wicked plots devised
under the guise of truth and justice
parading hypocrisy as democracy
using any means to bust us
keep us under subjection
soften our mental erection
until we are impotent
no longer able to reproduce the perfection
of pharaohs, kings, and queens
the dreamer nor the dream
not even a muse to inspire greatness
or a griot to memorize and verbalize
a million cases that prove we are not
born of inferior races
my people come forth from your tombs
and take this truth in hand

The time is come for your final stand
under my command let us wage this war
the choice is yours
live as slaves or die free
what is it to be?
the battle is upon us
let the archers bend their bows
let the cavalry charge our foes
the artillery strike their blows
our armies conquer those
who have dared to awaken
the anger of the gods
that the hammer of the gods
might fall upon one and all
who conspire to make us crawl
behold we are risen no more division
under the blazing sun
we will march as one

blacks who sang we shall overcome
descendants to the land of the rising sun
native americans who hunted the buffalo
chinese who built the railroads
brown men who pick the grapes of wrath
women who are our better half
children who need a brighter tomorrow
the oppressed of the world
who endure great sorrow

I am the watchman
who watches over all
the lover of your soul
to catch you when you fall
In your time of trouble
I will hear you when you call
deliver you when
your back's against the wall
now steady your hands
with my courage indispensable
cast off their lies
so reprehensible
know that their positions
are indefensible
and let us ride into battle
knowing this principle
we are, you are, I am
Invincible.

School Daze

One day while walking through the park
I overheard a young man holding court
he growled motha fuck this and goddamn that
and nigah, nigah, nigah, every chance he got
I politely interrupted saying, if you please
son, permit me to teach you life's ABC's

cause ignorance like your's is Askin' to be taught
and what you about to learn can never be Bought
you been foolin' your peers but now you bout to get Caught
you may Dread what i say but give it some thought
you can't Elevate yourself with your mind in the gutter
that's like using margarine when the recipe calls For butter

God is not a prefix for the word damn
and you on the road to Hell if you keep dissin' the man
his Infinite wisdom believe me you need to seek
cause when you refuse his mercy it's Judgement you reap
don't take my Kindness for weakness i'm just helpin' you out
cause Love knows you don't know what the hell you talkin' about

you call yourself a Man yet you act like a child
you call your friends Niggas and they so stupid they smile
you call yourself Oppressd but you're your own oppressor
don't Prepare for success, you'll always settle for lesser
if you Quit the race before the race is done
you just Runnin' for nothin' ain't no prize to be won

don't be Stupid cause the world takes advantage of fools
don't be a Thief cause what you steal will be stolen from you
don't be a User cause users only end up gettin' used
don't be a Victim cause victims waste their lives cryin' the blues
don't be a Wanna be if you wanna be known as a professional
cause a Xerox copy's never as good as the original

You act like an animal son believe me it's true
you'll end up doin' time in the motha fuckin' Zoo.

Revolutionary

I do the work of a stone revolutionary
stayin' true to the mission that the title carries
I'm not fighting to overthrow democracy
just ignorance lies and hypocrisy
my job to open the people's eyes
transform from foolish to wise
jumpstart the brain and get 'em thinkin'
get 'em off drugs and make 'em stop the drinkin'
clear the club of undercover mothers and Sadies
send 'em home determined to raise their babies
stop daddies from runnin' buck wild in the streets
bring 'em home to their families with groceries to eat

I'm not a rapper, a lyric slapper
a name dropper, hip-hopper, no
I'm A Revolutionary
I free the mind, give sight to the blind
expose the oppressors behind, behold
I'm A Revolutionary
linguistical cockroach, infesting generations
spreading across the nation, oh
I'm A Revolutionary
ignoring the bling, don't need critics to validate us
none but the righteous can infiltrate us
We're Revolutionaries

Politicians are all about gettin' your vote
slingin' up your neighborhood with political dope
tryin' to get the people high with change and hope
once elected slip away like soap on a rope
no more shakin' hands and kissin' babies
avoid the real people like plagues and rabbies
busy fillin' the pockets of political friends
til election time when it's time to do it again
to the preachers in the pulpit preachin' the truth
I support your vision and give a salute
but you schemers and skeezers using the steeple

to finance your lifestyle and fleece the people
you can fool some of the people some of the time
but you, I and God know you lyin'
just tellin' the sheep what they wanna hear
best be keepin' it real judgment day is near

I'm not a rapper, a lyric slapper
a name dropper, hip-hopper, no
I'm A Revolutionary
I free the mind, give sight to the blind
expose the oppressor's behind, behold
I'm A Revolutionary
linguistical cockroach, infesting generations
spreading across the nation, oh
I'm A Revolutionary
ignoring the bling, don't need critics to validate us
none but the righteous can infiltrate us
We're Revolutionaries

Don't lead your children to believe
a library's a video store
put a book in their hands a dream in their hearts
to strive for more
when teachers ask them what they want to be
when they mature
let 'em pull out laptops print flowcharts and say
an entrepreneur
teach them education's about more than quizzes
it's about life
encourage them to own businesses grab market shares
and cut a slice
it's not about rims, whips, or nigahs who can't spell
what they spit
it's about being your family's provider
and your paycheck being legit
making your mark in this world
don't mean spray painting the neighbor's garage
let them know all praise belongs to The Most High

for He opens doors
warn them not to end up cryin'
over the only job they qualify for
when you pleasure the body and neglect the mind
that's what life has in store
mistake a prison yard for a university campus
you gonna be in trouble
when reality drops the gavel
and burst your little gangsta bubble
you read a text message but not a textbook
you throwin' life away
there's a black man in the white house
wake up ya'll it's a new day

I'm not a rapper, a lyric slapper
a name dropper, a hip-hopper, no
I'm A Revolutionary
I free the mind, give sight to the blind
expose the oppressor's behind, behold
I'm A Revolutionary
liguistical cockroach, infesting generations
spreading across the nation, oh
I'm A Revolutionary
ignoring the bling, don't need critics to validate us
none but the righteous can infiltrate us
We're Revolutionaries

Teaching my teachers is a noble profession
preparing students for life is a wonderful blessin'
but I got to admit I got a confession
some of ya'll ain't worthy to be teachin' the lesson
preying on the minds of the young and the weak
contaminating their little heads with the garbage you speak
unlike real teachers who are true to the cause
some of ya'll usin' children to buy houses and cars
don't start complainin' cause I'm drenching you with lyrical rain
and it's washing away your lies and exposing your game
use my blanket of truth to cover your shame
then do an about face and start clearing your name

I wouldn't hit you if I thought you weren't built to take it
just saw you fallin' short and thought I'd help you make it
remember this lesson and you'll never have to fake it
life will always be whatever you make it

I'm not a rapper, a lyric slapper
a name dropper, a hip-hopper, no
I'm A Revolutionary
I free the mind, give sight to the blind
expose the oppressor's a$$ alas
I'm A Revolutionary
liguistical cockroach, infesting generations
spreading across the nation, oh
I'm A Revolutionary
ignoring the bling, don't need critics to validate us
none but the righteous can infiltrate us
We're Revolutionaries.

Listen

Man rises up
from his shallow bed
showers real quick
gets dressed and fed
kisses three grandchildren
on the head
scars on his hands
from the life he's led
30 years on a forklift
workin' that night shift
faithful as a dog when he's called
to his food dish
25 years married no decay
into the night he goes and she goes
back to pray

Listen to the rhythm of the rain
listen to the rhythm of the rain
to the rhythm
to the rhythm
to the rhythm, the rhythm, the rhythm

Sirens slicing through the night
lights blazin' like a sea
of black and whites
17-year-old face down in the street
gang victim
under a blood soaked sheet
momma behind yellow tape
weeping in vain
neighbors gather around
trying to ease her pain
old man says
with a hand on her shoulder
they dress like thugs
but they dyin' like soldiers
a whole generation goin' to waste

nothin' to show for it
but a homicide case

the lion's out on the prowl tonight
man searching for a girl
that will treat him right
swoops off the freeway exit
coal black Lexus
license plates all the way from Texas
slows to a crawl
when he hits the backstreets
Billy snow white
but he loves that dark meat
spots his prey
she grabs her pay
jumps in beside him and they drive away
same predatory story
from beginning to end
change the names and faces
then tell it again

Listen to the rhythm of the rain
listen to the rhythm of the rain

Eddie puts in a call to his girl Trudy
how bout you and me go catch a movie
getting out for Trudy's like a trip to heaven
please pick me up at a quarter to seven
drops the phone when dad ask
who was that
we only got two hours
before your momma's back
ten minutes early
Eddie knocks on the do'
she comes out walkin' funny
but she's ready to go
he says I'm early
wanna grab a beer
she says take me anywhere but here

they keep driven through the night
heading into the light

Rocket man Smitty
been three years clean
every day hits the sidewalk
lean and mean
knockin' on doors lookin' for work
comes home with nothin'
but the sweat on his shirt
seems everyone is firing
but nobody's hiring
finally the rejection gets so tiring
Smitty pawns the radio
gets himself a little dough
scores a little smack
in the back of the liquor store
thinkin' he's alone
finds a vein
ties it off
rams it home
junior wakes from his nap
soon the door swings open
like a human trap
Smitty stares into the eyes
of his wife and son
junior says
daddy show me how that's done?

Listen to the rhythm of the rain
listen to the rhythm of the rain

After 12 years of school
she can barely spell cat
never spoke in class
scared of being laughed at
odds for success
are a million to one
but her chance of gettin' pregnant

is bright as the sun
a matter of time
before the wall caves in on her
boys on the block
waitin' to lay their hands on her
tokens for her bus fare
food card and welfare
plus a baby girl
and all she had to do was lay there

I'm not perfect
Lord you know that
it's an everyday battle
just to keep me on track
but you promised to return someday
and with nail scarred hands
wipe our tears away
now I've read
where you said
all things are spiritual
not tryin' to rush you
but shit down here's critical
while meditating in the dark
he wrote his answer upon my heart
"Every time you see suffering
you want to heal it
but if you never let it touch you
how can you feel it?"

So listen to the rhythm of the rain
listen to the rhythm of the rain
to the rhythm
to the rhythm
to the rhythm, the rhythm, the rhythm

Grandpa gets home from nightshift
neck all sore and back stiff
grandma's leavin' for the dayshift
on her way out they exchange a kiss

sun peeking over hills
in through dusty blinds
shiny as a handful
of silver dimes
just before grandpa goes to bed
gets down on his knees
and bows his head
gives thanks for his job
and thanks for his life
ask protection for his grandkids
and his wife
turns off the light
climbs into bed
with ghetto birds flying
overhead

He listens to the rhythm of the rain
listens to the rhythm of the rain
to the rhythm
to the rhythm
to the rhythm, the rhythm, the rhythm
Listen.

The Way of the Chameleon

Spittin' fyah like dragons in fairy tales
trackin' frauds like hounds from hell
hunting down liars and the lies they tell
killing with truth that always prevails

Bangin' on busters
rainin' down justice
exposing the plots of
those who don't trust us
stompin' on fakers
chewin' Now or Laters
breaking the jaws of
the doubters and haters

Freeing people from taboos of the past
liberating artists from thieves who steal cash
teaching poets to kick literary a$$
puttin' fear under wheels and steppin' on gas

Born in the ghetto
sprung from a rat hole
trained by the streets and
ready for battle
armed with a lexicon
deadlier than Kubla Khan
gathering an army
to get the revolution on

Life's a war and I was born to fight
my style's invincible my flow air tight
don't need weapons to put enemies to flight
all I need is a solitary mic

Words like smart bombs
blowin' up ear drums
injecting brains with
love transfusions

shocking these zombies
out of their fantasies
bringing a message
to save humanity

Gathering an army numbering in the millions
making samurai out of ordinary civilians
ninja poets filling stadiums and pavilions
learning the way of linguistical chameleons

Stop chasing pipe dreams
life is not a flat screen
wake up from your nightmare
to the joy of living
rejuvenation
the beauty of creation
you don't have to buy
it's all across the nation

Break the spell of infectious advertisers
emancipate from the slavery of merchandisers
release the choke hold of political organizers
unplug the influence of media sanitizers

Put it in reverse now
family first now
give up your addictions
cause they only make it worse now
rise and be free now
all follow me now
make love today
cause there's no guarantee now

Rapidly approaching the destruction of man
the power to change is within our hands
time to execute the master plan
make the lion lay down with the lamb.

The Oracle

Like David anointed to be king
sovereign ruler of everything
only to find he's just a man
now too Lord I understand
I am but instrument in your hands
to wield my pen as you command
breathe into me the breath of life
make me Lord a shining light
a beacon guiding through the night
when I take up pen to write
pour out your heart upon my page
and help me not to turn away
from this cross I am born to bear
listen poets everywhere
if pen be mightier than the sword
let us now in one accord

Strike a blow, a blow for those
starving in refugee camps in Sudan
strike a blow, a blow for women
striving for freedom in Afghanistan
strike a blow, a blow for children
toiling in the sweatshops of South America
strike a blow, a blow for people
searching for equality in America
for God has placed within our hands
the mighty power of the pen
why then seek the praise of men
when every word does flow from Him
revolutions, the birth of nations began
in the mind of a poet and the power of his pen
through the ages it's the poet who speaks
for the poor, the oppressed, the aged, and weak
be you pacifist, humorist, classical or mod
a poet once inspired is the oracle of God.

The Loneliest Star

During a book signing
looked up to see two little eyes
I smiled at the girl
holding to her mother's hand
her mouth said
I know who you are
I asked, "so who am I?"
she whispered you that star
her mother added
keep teaching the truth
these baby's future
in your hands
to which all I could do was say
"yes mam"
that evening the girl's future
was still on my mind
when approached by a dealer
sayin' I got what you need
my lexicon locked and loaded
I removed my shades
and exploded
nah bruh, I don't think you do
but you'll have a new perspective
before this conversation's through
he said what that mean
you wanna make a buy
to which I responded
my woman, my words, and my creator
are my high
but since you introduced the subject
let's go head and break it down
I looked into your future my man
and let me tell you what I found

You got crack ladies
with crack babies
while you out

driven Miss Daisy's Mercedes
but who's gonna feed those children
when they momma's
pushin' up them daisies
all you junkies and users
rage at me if you can
though that's like
screamin' at a lifeguard
for trying to save a drowning man
say I'm preachin'
but I'm teachin'
with these words of truth
I'm reachin'
to try and save you from yourself
then maybe you'll save someone else
hear me jack
it's a fact
once you fall on your chin
it makes it seven times harder
to rise up again
from Persia to Greece to Rome
the great kingdoms of men
never fall from without
they always crumble from within
and all you grinders
slingin' dope
who keep tellin' yourself
if they don't get it from you
they'll get it from somebody else
only God can judge
so I'm just speakin' for myself
better to let their blood
be on the hands of that
somebody else
TRUTH
I don't need no choir to sing it
no deacons to say amen
long as I got breath
I'll sling it

just as fast as I can

How we gonna
rise up as a people
when we keep
knocking ourselves down
how we gonna go the distance
when we too high to last a round
I had to go from 0 to 60
in three seconds flat
to put my life in gear
and blow that monkey off my back
it takes conviction
but you can do it
in the blink of an eye
one day fallen down drunk
the next day sober and dry
I'm just mortal man
not a Jesus Christ
but a scripture a day keeps me
healthy, wealthy and wise
how many of the gifted
do we really have to lose
to turn our backs on the devil
and stop walkin' in his shoes
Charlie Parker, Jimi Hendrix
River Phoenix, Heath Ledger
we can be here all night
cause the list goes on forever

This truth
won't make me popular
and it won't bring me fame
and when I'm dead
only a few may remember my name
but if it helps one girl or boy
become a woman and man
if given half the chance
I'd do it all again

I ain't just fishin'
I'm on a mission
gotta work while it's day
cause who gonna listen
when I'm old and gray
women may love me
and brothers hug me
for the fyah I spit
but if it don't help somebody
to me it don't mean shit
nough said?
or do I need chop it up more
truth taught lesson learned
and I'm out the stage door
I'm called for a purpose
for me it's do or die
even if it makes me
the loneliest star in the sky.

Chapter Five:
The Flame That Never Dies

Show me a hero and I will write you a tragedy.

F. Scott Fitzgerald

Mandela

Umtata awake
Mvezo burst forth with song
tell the sun not to set
but only to turn it's eye upon the horizon
for up the road the king is coming
tell the lion to bow his head
and the bateleur to fly ahead
and alert all the villages
Rolihlahla is coming
Mandela is Free
spread the word
from the humble township of Cape Town
to the skycrapers of Johannesburg
from the rich manicured lawns
and wealth of Sandton
to the tin roofed shacks of Soweto
the Son of Freedom
and strong right hand of Justice
is on his way to bring democracy
to South Africa
on the head of his spear is Apartheid
its rancid blood dry and decaying
its memory fleeing into the bush
to be seen no more
tell the Thembu to prepare the feast
let the Xhosa nation rejoice
the son stolen from her
over a quarter century ago has returned
the free man was taken away a slave
but now the slave has returned as ruler
the freedom fighter has returned
with freedom draped over his shoulders
he has returned home victorious
his hair grayed but his head unbowed
he who was taken away in chains
has returned to break our chains
Mandela, Mandela, Mandela

Mandela is Free
and with him we are all free
tell South Africa it is a new day
a day when all men become equal
men as black as the fertile soil
beneath their feet
and men as white as the roving clouds
above their heads
are now both equal
are now both South Africa
are now both one nation
the prison of Robben Island
that has been his home
will be his home no more
just as the presidential palace
that has been home to apartheid
will be its home no more
tell the workers they need not
be out of the suburbs by sundown
tell your brothers and sisters
they no longer need a pass
to travel from township to township
in their own country
tell them they are no longer outcast
outsiders and strangers
in their own homeland
tell the children they can dream of more
than just working in the mines
put down your baskets my sisters
come out of the fields my brothers
line the roads of the villages
make yourselves thick
along the city streets
wave your hands
and raise your voices
until they rattle the peaks
of the Drakensberg Mountains
and ripple the waters of the Mbashe River
Mandela, Mandela, Mandela

Nelson Rolihlahla Mandela is free
South Africa is free
we are free.

Sleepless In Seattle

If only you could have
had a couple good nights of sleep
laid your head to rest
from all the turmoil and agony
roller skating around in your brain
and twisting your stomach into knots
a few peaceful nonstop nights and days
of unbroken solitude and tranquility
from the demons
that took refuge in your head
and peeled back your skin
one layer at a time
on an hour by hour basis
never finding what they were looking for
but nonetheless
continuing their sadistic search
until it drove you into the streets
and onto the streets
looking for a needle in a haystack
a haystack in a needle
that you could lie upon
and slip into blissful
unconsciousness if only for a moment
then, maybe then
you would not have been pacing
back and forth at this odd hour
weapon in hand
contemplating
weighing life and death in the balance
to see which offered more relief
a greater release
from this hell you've descended into

Smacked out one minute
pupils dilated
head in some ominous cloud
feeling as high as you kept the legions

who loved your music
loved you to the brink of worship
their love for you and your love for them
could have been nirvana
if not for the next moment
when your veins were wailing like sirens
stage lights and cameras flashing
as the razor blades of addiction
sliced through your skin
with a fury so maniacal
not even bashing your guitars
into splinters and obliterating
stages full of equipment
could silence the sounds
of the howling
the psychotic rasping of minions
laughing and urging you on
circling you like a human bonfire
watching their delirious flames
lick the flesh from your bones
then leave your skeleton dangling
like a musical marionette
strung up and strung out
in front of the millions
thrashing about in mosh pits
seeking to extricate themselves
from psychological tar pits of their own
lighting matches to celebrate
to coronate, and honor you
pledging their allegiance
to your biographical anthems
and the pain smeared agony and truth
that sprayed from your lips
down and out your fingertips
a truth their parents, their teachers
and the world wouldn't tell them
tried to hide from them
but you passed it out freely
threw it out from the stage

like guitar picks
stubble on your chin
strands of unattended hair
swinging back and forth like pendulums
across your face
eyes ablaze
and that quirky little grin of a smile
pulling a generation of outsiders
into your inner circle
winking at them to let them know
you know who they are
the emptiness they feel
and the obstacles they face
obstacles not unlike your own
when you walked the streets of Aberdeen
looking for your next meal
the next lumpy tattered sofa to crash on
the next drug to remind you
how to forget
and now here you are reminding them
how to forget

Fame becomes just another noose
you struggle to slip free from
while enduring months of tortured existence
punctuated by the occasional rehab
only to return to a pit deeper and darker
than ever
as if being punished for even the attempt
at untangling your life
from the umbilical chord
wrapped vomit tight around your throat
like a tourniquet
stopping the flow of blood
to your head but not your heart
a heart that is the mighty engine
fueling your massive genius
to touch the hearts of millions
of street urchins so much like you

that your gravel throated growl of a voice
became their voice
and your songs
became the soundtrack for their lives
until the clock struck midnight
encasing you in a blackness so thick
not even quiet thoughts
of the daughter you loved
could silence the agitating roar
that had you up at that hour pacing
unable to sleep
quarreling with the hissing and shrieks
trying to appease those sirens
pleading to be silenced
right up until the time
the recoil of your rifle
sent their voices
your genius and you
hurling into eternity
into nirvana.

The Gift

(for Michael)

Hatched onstage
pint-sized dynamo
wind him up and watch him go
whirlin' twirlin'
sing so sweet got women's toes curlin'
face cute as cupid
pops ain't stupid
may be a little green
but this kid's a money machine
make all the right introductions
hook up those motown connections
push the hit machine into production
sellin' this sweet pea will be
easy as ABC
don't need no schoolin'
kid's a natural
born to groove
silky smooth
whew! look at him move
stick him in a show
put him on the road
oops, there goes his childhood
how much we make tonight?
yeah, it's all good
pack him off for the next town
watch the kid throw it down
man he's a killer
a stadium filler
I'm tellin' you the boy's a thriller!
don't stop til we get enough kid
one more time
show me that little move you did
kid spent around landed on his toes
then backwards he slid
whew! you bad...

Butterflies are beautiful
especially in the spring
but there are those who get their thrills
from pulling off their fragile wings
why do we find it hard
to let such innocence fly free
could it be the tainted image we see
is really a reflection of you and me

Put him in the spotlight
an ant under a magnifying glass
burn off his antennae
fry his sense of direction
throw him to the wolves without protection
he exist for our satisfaction
everyone gets a piece of the action
except the main attraction
no graduations or proms
for a teen sensation
feed him standing ovations
and wild accusations
then watch with fascination
when he exhibits social retardation
surround him with handlers and panhandlers
and leeches
and people who love to make speeches
but when the lies begin
where are these friends?
they desert you like shark infested beaches
call you a lost cause
nail you to a cross
and leave you there to bleed
broken for all the world to see
show your crucifixion 24/7 on TV
people who never even knew you
line up to persecute you
call you a freak, a molester
laugh at you like the court jester

strip you of your innocence
your decency
hang your carcass on a tree
cameras become your mirrors
to dissect, inspect, infect
everything you do
make your world a zoo
and you
a clown in a three ring circus
your face now out of focus
you desecrate it
as if to choke us

Butterflies are beautiful
especially in the spring
but there are those who get their thrills
from pulling off their fragile wings
why do we find it hard
to let such innocence fly free
could it be the jaded image we see
is really a reflection of you and me

The Creator who gave us
this magnificent butterfly
sits on high and looks down low
sheds a tear because he knows
in our lifetime in this short time
never more will we behold
such a rare combination
of spirit, body and soul
we were gifted with his presence
for a moment in time
to amaze us and uplift us
bring some joy into our lives
show us magic in his movements
touch our hearts with his songs
show the innocence of a child
can last a whole life long
in his smile and his laughter

in his eyes and gloved hand
in his caring and compassion
and his daring imagination
we were treated to a glimpse
of the mirrored traits of God
who so saddened that His gift
to the world he created
was maligned and degraded
once again falsely accused
so the gift he reclaimed
and now this immortal soul
moonwalks through heaven
on transparent streets of gold
while the angels applaud him
and the host of zion sings
we on earth tainted and jaded
are left with those who pull off
butterfly wings.

The Trail of Tears

They say we must move
move from the land that has been
our home for as long as any can remember
for as long as clouds have gathered
above our heads
and the fertile soil has lay
beneath our feet
move away from the sacred places
where we have buried our ancestors
and the familiar grounds
where we have raised our children
move from where we have hunted
the buffalo and deer
from where we have planted
corn and rice
from where the lakes and rivers
and streams are plenteous
and provide us with fish to eat
and fresh water to drink
move from where our campfires
have lit the night sky like fireflies
and sent smoke twisting into the daylight
high above the trees
move from where we are happy
and our families and villages thrive
where the land has been good to us
and we are at peace with the earth
never taking from it what we do not need
and only asking of it what it desires to yield
still Jacksa Chula Harjo the great white father
says we must move

Oh Great Spirit
the white settlers rush down upon us now
like the locust stripping the land bare
they kill the buffalo for sport
they kill the beaver and the deer

for their fur and hide but waste their meat
always killing what they do not need for food
poisoning the waters with their
mills and factories
cutting down our forest
to build their towns and settlements
damming the rivers to make them go
where they do not wish to go
they sell my people whiskey
and when they are drunk
they steal their money
and trick them into signing treaties
that steal our land
treaties that only speak lies
and make promises
they do not intend to keep
and if we refuse to give up our land
they take it anyway
murdering our elders and children
killing and raping our daughters
mothers and wives
our brave warriors fight them
to protect what is ours
and to avenge the deaths of our people
who they stamp out like a campfire
no longer needed
but we cannot win this battle
for they are great in number
like the stars in the midnight sky
and we in comparison are few
they use their laws
which we do not understand
to cheat and defraud us
and when they cannot do that
they turn their long rifles
and cannons upon us
they place great value on their lives
and land and possessions
but they place no value on our lives

and land and possessions
Great Spirit you are fair
you honor truth and justice
judge the white for this evil and treachery
banish them back to where they came
that we may keep our land
that you have given us
continue our traditions of old
and be at peace with the life
you have given us

Oh Great Spirit
they have stolen our land
with unjust treaties and violence
and have driven us from our lodging places
the Cherokee, Chickasaw, Creek, Choctaw,
Natchez, and Shawnees from the Southeast
the Winnebago, Iroquois, Potawatomi, Algonquin
and Erie from the north and great lakes
the Delaware, Susquehannock, Penobscot,
Seneca, from the northeast
from the great plains the Osage, Pawnee,
Cheyenne, Iowa, Missouri and Omaha
all these and hundres of other tribes
and nations that you have given this land
are now being purged from it
with bayonets at our backs
our way of life traditions and sacred rituals
stripped from us like the bark from trees
and our fate scattered to the wind
like so many autumn leaves
our people are herded together like cattle
and made to walk for months
through the snow and cold of winter
many thousands of our people
especially the elderly and the children
die along the way from the freezing cold
and icy winds from which we have
no protection

they huddle us onto steamships
to move us across the great river
we are so crowded together that
one person's foot stands upon another
here thousands more die of diseases
that spread amongst the people like wildfire
sometimes wiping out entire tribes
on our long journey west
the whites take the treaty money we have left
by overcharging us for the blankets
tainted meat and rotting corn they sell us
many of our people die from starvation
on this forced journey
thousands more die from the spoiled food
we must eat to survive
the journey is hard and most of my people
are on foot and barefoot
our once proud people are now emaciated
ravaged by disease and hunger
haunted by the memories of loved ones
they have buried
beside the many nameless paths
they have traveled
their bones to be dug up
and remains feasted on by wild animals
where I once saw courage and bravery
wisdom and life
in the eyes of my people
now I see only fear and sickness
exhaustion and death
on this trail of tears
that stretches from our homeland
to the wasteland we must now call home
we were once strong and independent
but now we are broken and defeated
forced to put out our hands for crumbs
like beggars
Great Spirit
why have they made us to suffer

why have they stolen our land
and driven us to the point
where we are destitute and haggard
we have called you to our aid
why have you not come
why do we see only your back
and not your face
are your eyes blind to our suffering
are your ears deaf to our cries
is your heart closed to our fate

Oh Great Spirit
those of us who have survived
the arduous journey and eluded death
stand upon the parched and barren land
where the whites have placed us
a land that stretches out dry and thirsty
before us
it is land they have given us
because they do not want it
because it is waterless and useless
because it is unable to sustain life
and a blight upon the landscape
here there are no buffalo deer or beaver
no rivers and streams teaming with fish
no forest to provide wood or shelter
no fertile soil in which to plant our crops
or grasses on which to graze our cattle
no herbs for our medicine men
to make their medicines
no berries or nuts for our women to gather
no shaded places for our children to play
there is no history here for our old warriors
to recall past battles and victories
no future for our chiefs to plan
it is a land where our warriors
have no battles to fight
our hunters have no game to catch
and our chiefs have no nation to lead

our old land was full of life and laughter
but this is a place of death and sorrow
where dreams come to die

Oh Great Spirit
why are we banished to this wilderness
why are we abandoned
left to become a nation of drunken men
and weeping women
helpless elders and hopeless children
Great Spirit
show us your face
make us to prosper and flourish once more
bless us again with the buffalo and antelope
rivers lakes and streams
open grassy plains and campfires of old
do not let us perish from the earth
a broken and forgotten people
and if you will not do this
then give us the courage and warrior spirit
of Chief Osceola the Seminole
who the whites could never defeat in battle
and let us all die the death of proud warriors
Oh Great Spirit
do not let this trail of tears
have caused us to weep in vain.

Hallowed Ground

When you receive the rewards of your profession
bow your head to pay homage
and come calling with hat in hand
never letting yourself forget
how all these privileges and riches
came to be bestowed upon you
purchased by the blood, sweat and tears
of those who came before you
whose shoulders you now stand upon
footprints you now tread within
who endured the hatred and outlasted the disdain
of ignorant men and unjust laws
to win for you the freedom to excel
to exhale without the threat
of lynchings, martyrdom, or exclusion
it was they that pulled back the black curtain
that all might witness
the towering tenacity of your talent
the magnificence of your superior skills
the grace with which you stand
the speed with which you move
the power invested in your voice
the beauty constructed into your face
the sexiness compacted into your hips
breasts, thighs, lips and eyes

When you enter onto the field of play
every time you step between the white lines
remove your spikes
for the ground you stand upon is holy ground
green pastures once roamed by kings and pharaohs
named Robinson and Aaron, Mays and Clemente
Doby and Campanella, Gibson and Paige
it is they and hundreds more
that laid the foundation for you
that built this bridge from the rags
to the riches you now enjoy

that blazed the trail that leads
from the outhouse to your penthouse

When your face emblazons the silver screen
take a moment to kneel in the darkened aisle
and give thanks
for it would not have been possible
without the flickering images of your predecessors
had Hattie McDaniel and Sydney Poitier
Dorothy Dandridge and Josephine Baker
the Nicolas Brothers and Oscar Micheaux
even Stepin' Fetchit, Nick Stewart, Amos 'N' Andy
Stymie and Buckweat not opened the theatre door
for you to be introduced to the world
where would you be
never step from your limousine onto the red carpet
and imagine that you made the trip alone
for you are carried on the wings of matinee angels
shaded by the shadow of giants

 In every industry and worthwhile endeavor
they were there first paving the way
for you to follow and reap the benefits
of their labor and toil, humiliation and abuse
tragedy and triumph
they paid for your freedom
with their courageous assault on Fort Wagner
they paid for your civil rights
with bloody bus rides and the souls of their shoes
they paid for your right to vote
with four small caskets in Birmingham
and three bodies at the bottom of a Mississippi lake
would you be a doctor
without Dr. Charles Drew and Dr. Daniel Hale Williams
would you be an inventor without Garrett Morgan,
Madame C.J. Walker, and George Washington Carver
a publisher without Frederick Douglass
W.E.B. Du Bois or John H. Johnson
a chemist without Percy Julian, Patricia Bath

and Marie Daly
an educator without Mary McLeod Bethune
Booker T. Washington or Marva Collins
could you have enjoyed the fruits of freedom
without Rosa Parks, Fannie Lou Hamer,
and Thurgood Marshall

Put down your hip-hop boasts momentarily
lay aside your gold chains and Rolex watches
Bentleys and Rolls Royces
Beverly Hills and South Beach mansions
and pay respects to those that deserve your respect
for he who does not remember the past
is condemned to repeat it
I know God is the orchestrator of our emancipation
but God works through people
and oh what magnificent people he created
to go before us and bare our burdens.

Obama

Not in comfort
on the wings of a Lear jet
your ancestors arrived with mine
in the belly of a slave ship
wore the same chains
felt the same shame mine did
were sold on the auction block
just like mine were
slaved in the fields
sun up to sun down
like mine did
had the same dreams of freedom
in their heads that mine did
housed the same hope
in their hearts that mine did
that's what they have to know
to understand how I felt
to understand how i
could laugh and cry
at the same time
realizing this moment, this victory
was yours as much as it was mine

How do I spell hope
Obama. O-b-a-m-a
How so I spell pride
Obama, O-b-a-m-a
How do I spell change
Obama, O-b-a-m-a
How do I spell freedom
Obama, O-b-a-m-a

They'd have to live their lives
under the shadow of Jim Crow
be despised and ostracized
in every public place they go
stand beside their woman

and have a child call them boy
walk past white women
with their eyes to the sidewalk
or risk being lynched on the strength
of mere accusation
speak only when spoken too
be paid like half a man
when they do the work of two
pay the same fare but have to ride
in the back of the bus
rise and give their seat
whenever a white person ask
obey laws
they weren't allowed to vote for
clean floors in neighborhoods
they aren't allowed to live in
help build churches
they aren't allowed to worship in
bypass superior schools
to attend inferior ones
die on foreign battlefields
for freedoms they don't have at home
seek protection from police
while knowing they're on their own
to truly know what Obama means to me
to a nation of me's
to a continent, a race, a world of me's

Obama is Martin's dream turned reality
The answer to Malcom's by any means necessary
Medger's blood not shed in vain
the breaking of Nat Turner's chains
he is the resurrection of a million souls
lost in the passage
the revival of a thousand men hung from trees
the resuscitation of 10 million
retrieved from hopelessness
who now can truly believe in democracy

How do we spell hope
Obama, O-b-a-m-a
how do we spell pride
Obama, O-b-a-m-a-
how do we spell change
Obama, O-b-a-m-a
How do we spell freedom
Obama, O-b-a-m-a

He is our 3/5ths of a man made whole
he is the 154th Massachusetts
taking Fort Wagner
he is the negro leagues
outlasting the major leagues
he is Jim Brown
winning the Heisman trophy
he is every black in America
getting their 40 acres and a mule
he is the Tuskegee Airmen
being honored as war heroes
with a parade down Pennsylvania Avenue
he is the buffalo soldiers
having their faces carved on Mt. Rushmore
right beside Teddy Roosevelt's

He is Dorothy Dandridge's beauty
being the equal of Marilyn Monroe's
he is crack cocaine
not flooding the inner cities
he is attack dogs turning and biting
Bull Connor in the ass
and firemen high pressure hoses
spraying single servings of koolaide
on brothers and sisters instead of stinging water
civil rights marchers being beaten
with cotton candy instead of clubs
he is George Washington signing
the Emancipation Proclamation
instead of Abraham Lincoln

he is every wrong made right
every injustice brought to justice
every act of hatred and cruelty
denounced and reversed
every oversight and inequity repaid
he is freedom finally ringing
our ancestors risen and singing
and the tide at long last bringing
back to us the bread we cast upon
the waters so many generations ago
he is the invisible man finally made visible
through the courage of a nation
deciding to become indivisible

How do we spell hope
Obama, O-b-a-m-a
How do we spell pride
Obama, O-b-a-m-a
how do we spell change
Obama, O-b-a-m-a
how do we spell love
Obama, O-b-a-m-a

Know that you are celebrated
by lovers of freedom the world over
and If you ever need a better view
of this brave new world
Mr. 44th President
you can stand on our shoulders.

TRIBUTE

(to Earth, Wind & Fire)

Who would I have been without you
I would have been blind without you
when I was struggling to understand
your words taught me how to be a man
You taught me not to fear Evil
cause the power within me is Mighty Mighty
and long as i Keep My Head To The Sky
my life will be Ever Wonderful
you taught me life is All About Love
you kept me Yearnin', Learnin'
to find the girl of my Fantasy
the one from Jupiter who'd come to rescue me
you told me to love her with Devotion
you gave me the Reasons, the Reasons
to take a Love's Holiday
find our Wonderland in this Boogie Wonderland

Even, After The Love Is Gone
and I'm Feelin' Blue after Just Another Lonely Night
still I find I Can't Hide Love
cause like you said it shows On Your Face
you advised me to wear it with Pride
then you said to me Time Is On Your Side
so Let Your Feelings Show and I Betcha'
someone will confess I Think About Lovin' You
then you will Singasong yeah
Straight From The Heart for Love Goes On
and though you say you'll never love again
someone will surely Change Your Mind
even though breaking up is Fair But So Uncool
go ahead and Fan The Fire

I'm sayin' Earth, Wind & Fire
with your songs of life You Open Our Eyes
to See The Light navigate These Changing Times

flow at The Speed Of Love at The Right Time
Like a Burnin' Bush your voice was so Divine
you said C'Mon Children use your Magic Mind
Anything You Want with enough Imagination
will come to you In Time
I Can Feel It In My Bones this Electric Celebration
will spread like a rainbow Round and Round
know the Spirit you seek is written In The Stone
so don't waste Energy sittin' and Daydreamin'
wondering Could It Be Right or could it be wrong
Freedom Of Choice is laid out before you
this is your time your Moment Of Truth
the hour is now to start a love Revolution

Start finding solutions for This World Today
don't be a Victim Of The Modern Heart
don't be deceived cause The World's A Masquerade
Keep It Real and wear your Heritage proudly
show the world you're a Shining Star
don't let success derail your System Of Survival
don't hang your head when haters pull their Dirty tricks
always remember That's The Way Of The World
just keep on telling your Kalimba Story
for the creator above says to us Love Is Life
so Let Me Love You
Even If You Wonder, Every Now And Then
know that Love Is The Greatest Story
do all you do In The Name Of Love
and when his blessings pour upon you
don't forget to show some Gratitude

When you're weary find some time to Getaway
just Sailaway for a Tee Nine Chee Bit
to rediscover the Beauty of life
and if the mood strikes you Rock It
Maurice, Verdine, Philip, Johnny
Al, Ralph, Andrew, Fred, Larry
and brother Charles Stepney
just want you to know i Can't Let Go

you've written so many songs for me
but tonight I'll Write A Song For You
when we meet on the other side of Lady Sun
stand in the almighty presence of the King Of Groove
whether Saturday Nite or Sunday Morning
june, july, august, or September
Remember The Children remember your lessons
and let our joy bring you a Happy Feelin'

when we Sparkle with the glow of Serpentine Fire
and all gather to pay you tribute
There's only one way to pour out our thanks
and that's simply to say brothers... Let's Groove.

Gifted Hands

(for Dr. Benjamin Carson)

Life and death
in the power of your hands
in the skill of your gifted hands
in the brilliance of your mind
in the faith you lean on
in the God you pray to
in the love that motivates you
and yet your story is not told daily
is not proclaimed from the rooftops
is not serenaded in song
or immortalized in operas
danced by ballet companies
or played by symphonies
how can this be?

A book yes, a movie even
but the miracle that is your life
should be required reading and viewing
for every inner city student
in every school in America
and even throughout the world
on day one of class every teacher
should be required to tell and retell
your amazing story to every student
students who will be blessed to hear
how you, labeled as dumb and ignorant
written off as unteachable, unreachable
thrown on the scrap heap by most
but thank God not all
rose to become the world's greatest
and most celebrated neurosurgeon
renowned around the globe
not for shooting a basketball
hitting a baseball or running with a football
but for performing the most difficult surgeries

any human being can perform
surgeries even other masterful surgeons
dare not perform, and most times succeeding
Separating conjoined twins
whose brains are fused together
surgically disconnecting them
then having the skill and knowledge
the stamina to stay on your feet
8, 12, 22 hours straight not wavering
as you reconnect God's delicate
and intricate circuitry
while listening to the classical music
you love, beneath your scalpel
tiny lives in your gifted hands
their lives, motor skills, speech, sight
all dependent
on micro-inches of movements
by those gifted hands
and still you do not falter
you do not flinch or lose focus

Schools should salute you every morning
Dr. Benjamin Carson
we should all salute you
as a shining, lasting example
of what every student can achieve
when they put the miraculous apparatus
called the brain to work
when they trust in the power
who gives them power
and dedicate themselves to excellence
and to the betterment of themselves
and all mankind
the loss of your children in birth
spurred your vast heart onward
to comfort and save our children
the great anger that raged within you
as a youth became greater love and compassion
the tragedy your life could have been

became the triumph it is
let your life be a lesson for us all
to never give up on a child for indeed
every child is crafted and molded
by gifted hands.

The Tree

From the tree was built vessels
that sailed upon the open seas
with human cargo out of Africa
bound for the hell of slavery
from the tree was carved the desk
on which Lincoln signed the proclamation
to break the chains of degradation
and set free a black nation
from the tree hangs the bitter fruit
that will forever stand
as a brutal symbol of man's
inhumanity to his fellow man
and from the tree was formed the gavel
that put an end to segregation
in the landmark case we know as
Brown versus the Board of Education
The tree, the tree, the tree, the tree

From the tree was made the frame
Rembrandt used to feature
the curious little smile
of his lovely Mona Lisa
from the tree fell the apple
that stirred Newton's calculations
and set in motion his brilliant mind
to solve the mystery of gravitation
from the tree was built the plane
the Wright Brothers did fly
above the plains of Kitty Hawk
to forever conquer the sky
and from the tree was fashioned the bats
swung by Aaron swung by Ruth
to write their names in baseball history
and become the legends of our youth
The tree, the tree, the tree, the tree

From the tree was shaved the arrow
that supplied Native American tribes with meat
until the rifle was manufactured
and made that arrow obsolete
from the tree was built the wagons
that carried pioneers on their quest
out of crowded eastern cities
to conquer the wild and spacious west
out of the tree were raised schoolhouses
to educate the minds of our nation's best
out of the tree came books and pages
that chart the course of their progress
and into the tree are carved initials
of starry-eyed lovers in the spring
who pledge love and devotion ever
no matter what the future brings
the tree, the tree, the tree, the tree

From the tree was plucked the fruit
in the garden known as Eden
to introduce the stain of sin
that leads us down the road to ruin
from the tree came the cross
where my savior bled and died
crown of thorns upon his head
blood streaming from his precious side
from the tree was birthed the pages
that unite and divide the nations
by the power of the words written
from Genesis through Revelations
and from the tree will grow the leaves
for the healing of the nations
when heaven does receive us home
from all our trials and tribulations.

Chapter Six:
Good Like Gumbo

Always get what you want
or you'll never want what you get.

Tensiongentry

Gimme The Mic

I'm kickin' back waitin' my turn
while these blase' poets
talk about flowers and autumn leaves
and the beauty of the trees
don't get me wrong I love Shakespeare
but that dude ain't up in here
what's this fascination
why all the John Muir imitations?
you Oppies raisin' more hopes
than your skills can carry
it's gettin' scary
this place is lookin' like a cemetery
man yall puttin' folks to sleep
with the boring way yall speak
dull and monotone
folks is sneakin' out and goin' home
before we all alone
step back Oppie and let me bring it on!

Gimme The Mic
I'ma shonuff killa
gimme the mic
I'ma word gorilla
gimme the mic
I'ma rock this bed
wake the sleepin' and raise the dead
smack 'em upside the head
with a verbal stream
rhyme 'em up, twist 'em up
til they wet their dreams
serve my poetic feast til everybody's fed
then send the boys home
and put the girls to bed

Yeh, I'ma heat 'em up
eat 'em up
spit 'em out

make 'em run to the dictionary
to understand what i'm talkin' bout
grab 'em by the earlobe
pour in some lyrical drano
unplug they ears open they minds
pull down they pants
and kick 'em in they academic behinds
twirl 'em with my style
flip 'em over a pile
of sonnets, couplets, syntax
hold my Starbucks homey
while I spit dat, yeah!

Now that I got the mic
see how the dead come to life
professor passin' round his peace pipe
the divorce's dancin wit his wife
feet are tappin' hands are clappin'
step away Oppie I ain't done flappin'
enee, menee, minee, mo
I got this dawg the rest of yall can go

Hey baby doll in the red dress
when God made you he didn't make no mess
girl you built like the Holland tunnel
open yo mouth and pretend my tongues a funnel
yo curves make me wanna take a drive
if you was a pool i'd take a dive
swim around in you for hours
if I was a garden i'd grow you flowers
yeh, keep smilin' it's all like that
yo old man don't like it
my car is parked out back
I'll take you to the Ghetto Saloon
fly you to the moon
soon as i'm through settin' fire to this room
You in the pinstriped vest
that babe you talkin' to ain't gon settle for less
now that she's seen the best

you still markin' on scantrons
when I invented the test
hear's a tic tac for your breath
don't bother to hang around
when I get through wit her won't be nothin' left
I'll wine her dine her
make her scream
like the whistle of an ocean liner

And yo, who prepared this food
was you jokin' or just being cruel
this mess is awful
makin' food this bad should be unlawful
somebody phone out for some Roscoe's
chicken and waffles
with a Fatburger on the side
wash it down with some red kool aide
chase it with some peach cobbler pie
girl don't sweat the calories
cause you and me
gonna find a dance club
where we can shake it off
then come back to my place
where we can take it off
now this poetry readings jumpin' off
where's the stereo
I feel a party comin' on
throw on some Marvin Gaye
yeh, Let's Get It On
you never heard poetry like this befo?
if you like the way I hustle and flow
get yourself out on the flo'
where this came from there's plenty mo
lean into me girl and shake it
now bend over and let me spank it
and slide, and slide, and slide
then hold it...

I got skills homey

I can stimulate, titillate, lubricate, vaginate
blow prose in they ears
til they damn near ejaculate
captivate, motivate, educate, pontificate
stick 'em on the end of my sentences
and spin they heads like dinner plates
spread a love poem so deep and wide
make the Klan and black muslims
wanna live side by side
make republicans start includin' me
make my enemies stop booin' me
make yo grandma think about doin' me
make gangstas feel warm and fuzzie
make 'em fear me like suggie
make the Pope wanna boogie woogie
I can spew rhymes like Moby
fly verses through the air like Kobe
you don't know me, i'm a bad man
I can turn a laureate into a coward
knock a crowd out the park like Ryan Howard
I can spit a million rhymes away
and still have enough left for a rainy day, Rah

Enjoyed yall but the clock is tickin'
gotta get cross town pretty quick and
if you ever need me again
I'm in the yellow pages
under Lyrical Assasin
let your fingers do the walkin'
then pick up the phone and start talkin'
100, 200, 300, four, except you baby girl
just look out yo window cause I'll be stalkin
now power to the people
I'm up outta here
so raise yo fists in the air
and wave 'em like you just don't care, yeh

Gimme The Mic
I'ma shonuff killa

gimme the mic
I'ma word gorilla
gimme the mic
I'ma rock this bed
wake the sleepin' and raise the dead
smack 'em upside the head
with a verbal stream
rhyme 'em up, twist 'em up
til they wet their dreams
serve my poetic feast til everybody's fed
then send the boys home
and put the girls to bed
yehhhhhhhhhhhhhh, gimme the mic!

Spittin' Fyah

I bust through the do'
they on me
folks flockin' to the show
they know me
all eyes on the stage
they waitin'
just to be amazed
anticipatin'

And i'm stalkin' back stage
like a lion in a cage
like a demon in a rage
the legend grows and grows
ready to add another page
to the history of prose

Someone hits the lights
they see my face and
I grab myself a mic
we off and racin'
they on they feet
I'll take 'em higher
hit the stage with fyah
burnin' like a train of desire

My words like lazers
sharper than razors
shockin' like tazers
everyone up and singin'
ladies screamin''
men sayin' i must be dreamin'
to be up in here watching the Pharaoh
of words slingin'

I'm paintin' pictures
with the colors i spit
i'm quotin' scriptures

got demons bout to sh-it
i'm gettin' sexy
got women throwin' panties
the audience is meltin'
like cotton candy

The stage is rockin'
hope it don't break
I keep 'em movin'
two hours straight
i got 'em runnin'
up and down the aisles
shoutin' water, water, water
the man's on fire

And I'm burnin' up the haters
and i'm burnin' perpetrators
when the walls start to shake
from my prophetic tongue
there's no escape
and i'm filling folks with hope
and i'm filling folks with faith
showing them it's not too late
to start tearin' down
the walls of hate

The blind are seein'
the mute are talkin'
the deaf are hearin'
the lame are walkin'
it's a literary miracle
my words of truth
are spiritual

I'm speaking visions of things to come
uniting all nations into one
destroying the hatred that divides
leading people to the light

teaching boys how to be kings
raising girls to be queens
sewing families back together
raining poetic manna from heaven

As i bow and turn my back
they goin' crazy
the stage goes black
that's why they pay me
I'm movin' through the pack
they wanna touch me
the limo's out back
let's get comfy
inside i collapse
i gave my all
give the Father snaps
i had a ball
we hit the interstate
the motor's hummin'
a sellout crowd awaits
they know i'm comin'.

Oh No He Didn't

Black Raven? Black Fool! Now you should know better
but I'll give you a moment to get yourself together
pretending you spittin platinum when you really spittin' hay
and thinkin' your tired rhymes make it somehow ok
don't ever dream of approachin' me with that hooked on phonics sh-it
I'm like Ali in his prime boy I'll make yo a$$ quit
I'm the master, the maestro, the poetic PH.d
and you dare to step to me with your G.E.D
you sound like someone tryin' to convince himself
cause you damnnnn sure ain't convincing nobody else
I'll run circles round your pathetic a$$ in my sleep
I'll spit so much fyah up yo a$$ your balls will melt from the heat
here's a blindfold, tell me how you want to die
and being a gentleman I'll do my best to comply
death by Shakespeare with some "to be or not to be"
death by Gordon Parks under "The Learning Tree"
death by Langston Hughes, Dylan Thomas, or Amiri Baraka
or maybe Darth Vader, Han Solo, or your girlfriend Chewbacka
from Churchhill to Lauryn Hill I can quote them all
so just tell me where, when and how you wanna fall
or would you rather I stoop down to your level of play
and throw some "see spot run" on your a$$ today
to go against someone of my caliber you ill equipped
if even the thought of testin' me runs through your mind slap that sh-it
cause knowing your A, B, C's is not enough to battle
thinkin' you can out spit me when you cain't even out spit my shadow
you had me laughin' at that playdo you thought was hard
but I stopped when I realized you're a poetical retard
it's not good manners to laugh at a literary handicap like you
so I'll break it down real slow Einstein so you can get a clue
supercalifragilisticexpialidocious
if you've read any of my work you'd know that I'm ferocious
you can't defeat a samurai by being bragadocious
especially when the lines you spit reek of halitosis
yeh, cat rhymes with bat, rhymes with hat, rhymes with mat
but you should be embarrassed spittin' out rhymes like that
when I'm like Kobe, Lebron and Jordan rolled into one

you against me ain't a battle boy it's a dunk-a-thon!!!
Alright, let me stop I see that you cryin'
wipe your tears at least your girl thinks you're a man for tryin'
and speakin' of your girl after I did her and she was layin' on my chest
she told me why your nickname lover boy is "10 seconds or less."
next time you wanna battle me I suggest a deserted island
cause it hurts a lot less to get your a$$ kicked in private!!!

Coyote Girl

She is the juice of a wild berry
the wind rustling autumn leaves
the scent of a desert rose
the gurgling of a stream over stones
the buzz of humming bird wings
the shadow under an elm tree
the silence of a butterfly
morning dew on the meadow

She is the tail of a streaking comet
the twinkle of a distant star
the crystal blue of a summer day
the prism of an arching rainbow
the fiery orange of a sunset
the line that marks the horizon
the blackness of midnight
a sunbeam peeking through clouds

She is a winding mountain trail
an echo in a deep canyon
the crackling of a campfire
the footprints of a gazelle
the smoke curling from a chimney
the yelp of a lone coyote
she is my desert love unspoken
and i am the whisper hidden in her heart.

They Look To Me But I...

Like Moses stretching forth his staff
to split the waters in half
Lead me Lord by your precious hand
that i might be a man
eviction notice in hand
tellin' us we gotta go even though
we have no other place to call home
through the wilderness we'll roam
unless you can provide
and if you do i'll step aside
better to swallow my pride
than see my wife and children on the streets
please hear my plea
even though you see
the wicked things i say and do
i'm a sinner of the worst sort
i know my prayer is short
but the clock is tickin' so could you be quick and
tear down these Jericho walls
that keep me from getting a decent job
you know i'll work hard
if someone would just give me a try
excuse me if i cry
but you're my only hope
don't let me go back to sellin' dope
to make ends meet
that would only lead me back to jail
and i've been through that hell
they say you can do anything but fail
oh well, the sheriff's knockin' on the do**
sayin' we gotta go so if you got a plan
please let me know cause my wife and children they

They look to me but i
can't change water into wine
they look to me but i
can't bring the dead back to life

they look to me but i
can't drown my problems in the Red Sea
they look to me but i, but i, but i...

Like the woman accused of sexual sins
in the midst of angry men
show me a way out
before these stones tear into my skin
poverty is all i've known
what do i own?
but the clothes on my back
please tell me that
there's more to life than what i see
barely seventeen
was i to tell
love from lust lies from truth
will the mistakes of my youth
follow me my whole life through
Lord what shall i do
now that he is gone
i'm on my own
raising two children all alone
is getting the best of me
I try to be all they need
but working and going to school
forgive me if i cry
it cuts like a knife
seeing them do without
fills me with doubt
would they be better left
on someone's doorstep
how much can i take?
every day i wake i'm about to break
gas turned off yesterday
today rent is due
how will we make it through?

They look to me but i
can't make the waves be still

they look to me but i
can't feed thousands with one meal
they look to me but i
am not the way, the truth, the life
they look to me but i, but i, but i...

Like the Apostle Paul imprisoned in Rome
the time of my departure is at hand
i've fought a good fight
now death is coming like a thief in the night
i feel his grip
and one day soon I'll slip
away from this life
my troubles will be over
i'll lift burdens off my shoulder
and lay them at your feet
victory will be sweet
no more of this cancer
that's eating me
this pain will soon be gone
i'm moving on to a better place
can't wait to see your face
you've been my strength Lord
when i'm too weak to stand
you hold my hand assure this man
heaven is my home when i leave
this world of confusion
gonna be a reunion
in the bye and bye
can't wait until i fly
look into the eyes of my dear wife
i've missed her so
you know she was my life
the loneliness i've felt
is about to melt into eternity
and when i'm free watch over my family
i've been their provider
they'll miss me but give them peace cause

They look to me but i
can't be their shepherd like you can
they look to me but i
can't lead them beside still waters and
they look to me but i
can't walk them through this valley of death
they look to me but i, but i, but i...

Finally, like John on the isle of Patmos
no one here but us
just you and me
tell me what to right
Lord guide my hand
help me understand
your purpose and your plan
bend my words right make my flows tight
i'll be your feet and hands
go where you send me
write what you give me
so give me the patience
to shake this nation wake this nation
cause Lord it's sleepin'
while the enemy is creepin' to and fro
don't they know
it's only you Most High
that stays the hand of disaster
the world is spinnin' faster every day
consumed by greed and hate
if you ask me progress is regress
help us make this mess what it should be
make our leaders see
it's not them but thee oh Lord
that holds our future in your hands
make them say amen
and guide this nation back to truth
don't let us go astray
help us find our way to be
One Nation Under God and when you do
from the time I exit the womb til I enter the tomb

i'll sing your praises cause no one else amazes that's why

They look to me but i
know you're the Alpha and Omega
they look to me but i
know you're the creator my savior
they look to me but i
know no one else can pull us through
they look to me but i
i look to you.

First Crush

You were my third grade teacher
beautiful and graceful
I watched you at the chalkboard
mesmerized by the way you moved
the curvaceous frame
that filled your clothes
sometimes you'd look up from your desk
and catch me staring
you'd smile and I'd shyly turn away
only to stare again moments later
I couldn't stop myself
the school bell would ring
and we'd all file past you out the door
I'd say goodbye with deep sincerity
and you'd pat me on the head
but even the humiliation of this
could not stop me from loving you
wanting to kiss you on the mouth
lay beside you in the sandbox
and tell you the things I'd do
once I became a man.

The Reunion

Funny what a day can bring
who'd have thought tonight I'd see
you on the arm of another man
me and another woman hand in hand
last time I saw you I was sayin' goodbye
and you were sayin' don't bother to write
it was the death of a love affair
we both pretended we didn't care
strange to see you with someone else
after having you all to myself
just you I and the stereo
the smell of love and the candle glow

Now this stranger to my eyes
is introducing us like you and I
don't know each other inside out
never made each other scream and shout
he don't know I know your sweet spot
we share a history that's so hot
you told me no one ever did you better
your love's so good made me run for shelter
I got your name on my bicep tell this guy
you got mine tattooed on your right thigh
but we pretend we don't know each other
be kind of awkward to say we were lovers

He says somethin' bout the economy
I nod my head and pretend to be
interested in this dude's book
when all I see is how good you look
my date ask if you like sushi
you answer somethin' about Gucci
my date and yours applaud the band
they walk on stage and begin playin'
one of those old school jams
people start to dance as the band plays

Ain't no mountain high enough
ain't no valley low enough
ain't no river wide enough
to keep me from getting' to you

Embers I thought had died reignite
like fireflies of love take flight
annoyed my date tugs at my sleeve
says this dude is talkin' to me
I hear him ask somethin' about the weather
but all I know is when we were together
your legs would wrap around my waist
my hands would hold your hips in place
my date says somethin' about real estate
I wonder how I let you slip away
all those years lost to foolish pride
now that you're standing near me I

Feel my heart thumpin' head reminiscin'
how good it felt when we were kissin'
this dude must have asked another question
cause everyone's looking in my direction
but their faces disappear from view
when I realize you want me too
I'm sensing now that our cover's blown
we're sliding back into the love zone
my date and yours are telling us both
somethin' bout you and I standing too close
I'm looking in your eyes and you in mine
beginning to feel like old times as the band plays

Ain't no mountain high enough
ain't no valley low enough
ain't no river wide enough
to keep me from getting to you

Whether karma, fate, or destiny
some people are just meant to be
my date ask if I can take her home

yours ask if he can speak to you alone
we look at each other and begin to laugh
surrendering to a love that never left
I pull you close and we begin to sway
my date storms off and yours walks away
we're dancing to this jam cheek to cheek
you whisper baby tell me somethin' sweet
I say once I was lost but now I'm found
we begin to get down as the band plays

Ain't no mountain high enough
ain't no valley low enough
ain't no river wide enough
to keep me from getting to you.

Something Wicked

(dedicated to Ray)

The sky is blue but clouds are rushing in
birds wing their way toward the safety of the trees
deer climb for higher ground with panicked eyes
Morgan Patrick hurries horses in from the field

as his daughter waits
and the wind blows
and the dogs bark
and the cock crows

suddenly the sky changes from blue to gray
a frigid wind comes ripping through the trees
rain begins to fall and the creek begins to rise
the smell of snow rides upon the wind

something
wicked
this
way...

The sky turns black as Nat Turner's hands
the angry rain pounds its fist into the ground
the impatient wind whistles and groans
Morgan closes and bolts the barn door

as the ground shakes
and the wind blows
and the dogs howl
and the cock crows

the sky turns blood red and rains down hail
the river overruns its banks and threads the corn
the barn door is torn off and sucked into the clouds
Morgan's hat flies as his daughter pulls him inside

the ground quakes
and the wind screams
and the dogs whine
and death rides on the wind

the milk white sky blankets the valley below
out of the blizzard comes something dressed in black
his hat secure and his coat tails perfectly still
Morgan and Meghan watch from the kitchen window
the man in black covering a mile with every stride
he hovers at the window dubs his hat and smiles
Morgan runs to his rifle on the rack above his bed
the man in black takes his daughter by the hand

Something
wicked
this way
comes.

Down Home Blues

Gimme soma that coffee you brewin'
gimme soma that tobacco you chewin'
gimme soma them eggs you cookin'
gimme soma them fish you hookin'
gimme soma those big words you use
and give me some of that Down Home Blues

gimme soma those flowers you pickin'
gimme soma those stamps you lickin'
gimme soma that paper you readin'
gimme soma that chicken you eatin'
gimme soma them Jeopardy clues
and give me some of that Down Home Blues

gimme soma that whisky you drinkin'
gimme soma those thoughts you thinkin'
gimme soma that grass you growin'
gimme soma that leg you showin'
gimme back soma my union dues
and give me some of that Down Home Blues

gimme soma that wood you stackin'
gimme soma them clothes you packin'
gimme soma those biscuits you bakin'
gimme soma that money you makin'
hand me soma those 2x2s
and give me some of that Down Home Blues

don't gimme none of those beans you burnin'
don't need none of those lessons you learnin'
don't gimme none of those tears you cryin'
don't gimme none of those lies you lyin'
don't won't none of that swine flu
just give me some of that Down Home Blues

gimme soma them nuts you crackin'
deal me soma those cards you stackin'
gimme soma that cake you bakin'
gimme soma that ass you shakin'
gimme somethin' I can use
and that's some of that Down Home Blues.

They Asked 4 It

(battle rhyme thread)

What fool done messed up and passed me the mic
knowin' damn well my flow is tight
you dare to stand next to me like you a star
that's like a flashlight standin' next to a Quasar
even yo mamma know better than to challenge me
hear her screamin' in the background
please don hurt mi babyyyyyyyyyyy!
you step to me son it's swim or die
I flow like the M-i-s-s-i-s-s-i-p-p-i
I'll raise your consciousness
and pinch your little nipples
pull down yo pants
and expose yo dangling participles
my heat'll hit you so hard
you'll misplace your modifiers
I'll yank out your tired rhymes
with my poetical pliers
how yall gonna stand before the king
sounding like boyscout campers
when I'm a grown ass poet
and yall still wearin' pampers
don't jump in the way of the Tension Express
get off the track boyz
or end up with a hole in your chest
I'm a killa, the seat filler, a word guerilla
I'll finish you off faster than salmonella
now that Michael's gone R.I.P.
I'm the Thriller
my verbal blows will be hittin' yo ass so quick
you'll think you the villain in a Bruce Lee flick
when you was battling them lightweights
you was the schoolyard bully
but now you fightin' a man
and I'm spankin' that booty
all yo fake bravado about Nines and Glocks

you wouldn't know real heat
from Flava Flav's clock
when I'm through wit choo fools
you'll be coughin' up blood
sayin' "how come nobody told me
this dude's that good?
his flow so tight and his style so refined
make me wanna stalk him
just to kiss his behind!"
now run tell momma
you got yo ass whupped again
and she can see details at 11 on CNN.

Great Expectations

The moment I exit the womb
the subtle trap is laid
I must erase the mistakes
generations have made
from my first awkward steps
relatives and relations
put a yoke round my neck
made of great expectations
setting goals in the sky
always just out of reach
got me stuck in the sand
like a whale on a beach
everyone in my life's
got a well prepared speech
their intentions are good
but their motives are weak
if it's all for my good
why is my heart full of gloom
why do I feel so alone
even in a crowded room

They swear it's not about them
that it's all about me
so why the disappointing stares
when I try to break free
if it's not about them
who the hell's it about
they say they're here for support
but I'm having my doubts
cause every time I do me
someone gets in the way
when I think for myself
there's always hell to pay
they say I'm smothered in love
but it feels like suffocation
my role's so tightly defined
I'm dying of strangulation

why expect of me
the things they couldn't do
I can barely do me
where'd I find the strength to do you
all your jumping up and down
is clouding my vision
your demands only lead me
to make bad decisions
why can't you just go away
and let me live my own life
if you can't keep your hands off the wheel
I'll pull over and you drive
I have my own goals to reach
I have my own way to strive
it's not your life support system
that's keeping me alive
I'd rather die in pursuit
of my own standing ovations
than live the rest of my life
chasing your great expectations.

The Great I Am

He
rolled the stars like dice
across the midnight sky
polished them like diamonds
and caused them to shine
hung the sun dead center
and set it ablaze
to give light and shed warmth
in the midst of our days
put the moon in place
to reflect the sun's light
like a torch above the earth
to guide us through the night
filled the vast oceans
from shore to horizon
raised mountains carved valleys
and made paths to find them
put cattle in the fields
in waters fish of all kinds
brought us inventions and technology
from the world's greatest minds
turned rain into rivers
to give us water to drink
then made those rivers
flow out into the sea
grew us beautiful flowers
all the plants and trees
gave me eyes so their beauty
I could clearly see
made the birds to fly
then gave them a song
gave me ears so I can hear them sing
all the day long
blew his breath of life into me
made me a living being
sustains this life with the blood
that courses through my veins

gave me hands to grasp
and arms to reach
gave me legs to run
and let me stand on two feet
gave me a mind to think
and a mouth to speak
gave me strength to chase the vision
I so desperately seek
gave me fruits, grains, vegetables
and plenty to eat
gave me wood from the trees
to build places to sleep
put a dream in my head
and hope in my heart
created someone who will love me
until death do us part
and as if all this
wasn't enough to be done
gave me life eternal
by sacrificing his son
wow!
He.

CPSIA information can be obtained at www.ICGtesting.com
Printed in the USA
LVOW122341260313

326167LV00003B/14/P